Archangels
Ascended Masters
and Divinities

Guide to Working with Divinities

D1253869

Other books by this author

Archangel's, Ascended Master's, God's, Goddesses and
Affirmations
©Khadija Franklin 2019
Proclaiming Your Birthright: Affirmations
©Khadija Franklin 2020

Archangels
Ascended Masters
and Divinities

Guide to Working with Divinities

KHADIJA FRANKLIN

Cover and Logo Design: Raymond Wade

A NOTE
FROM THE AUTHOR

To God, my guides, the archangels, ascended masters, gods, and goddesses... with eternal gratitude and appreciation for Your Divine Love, guidance, and support. Thank You.

Archangels are extremely powerful angels who help us and who oversee the guardian angels.

An ascended master is a great healer, teacher or prophet who previously walked upon the earth, and who is now in the spirit world helping us from beyond. Ascended Masters come from all cultures, religions and civilisations; both ancient and modern.

Their role is to help us connect to God and the universe, to find the true beauty within ourselves and help us harness the light within. Whether we believe in them or not is irrelevant to them; they care only that we become the absolute best of ourselves and help this world flourish into a place of light and beauty.

They work with everyone who calls upon them, whether you believe in God or not.

They will never violate the free will God bestowed upon us. Therefore, we must ask for their help before they can intervene.

I have written this book to help you understand Who's Who and which Divinities to work with for each particular situation and also affirmations to connect us with each Being.

Like many people I have met, I was confused about the identities and functions of the Divinities.

I have only mentioned the Divinities I have connected and worked with in this book. There are many more Divinities that I have not mentioned, mainly because I have not worked with them yet.

The Divinities described in this book are real. If you are new to working with them, or you are skeptical about their existence, you will soon find that this book calls upon the great Divinities to be your support and by your side.

A word of advice: Be sure to only ask the deities to help you with tasks associated with Divine love. If you ask them to fulfill a request involving revenge or acrimony, the negative energy will bounce back to you, but it will be magnified.

If you are angry with someone, it is best to ask the divinities to create a peaceful solution for the good of all.

Remember, we are all Divine Beings learning in different space to evolve our souls.

Regardless of your lifestyle or whether you are spiritual or religious, the Divinities help everyone who calls upon them. They are here to enact God's plan of world peace, one person at a time. They can help an infinite number of people simultaneously, while having a uniquely personal experience with each individual.

K.F.

INTRODUCTION

A trip from New York to London in 2011 changed everything for me. As I was waiting to board the plane, I heard a voice – out of nowhere – repeat three times: "*The Secret*". This triggered a memory I had forgotten from two months earlier: a lady I met at a spa, had told me all about this book called, "The Secret", by Rhonda Byrne. With haste, I went to the airport bookshop and asked them if they sold a book called, "The Secret." I was in luck, and I spent the entire plane journey reading it. What was revealed to me astounded me; knowing I could work with the universe and manifest what I want was unbelievable and incredible. As I began reading the book, my mind continually repelled the words as disbelief engulfed me. However, I persisted.

By the time the flight landed, I had finished the book. And yet, my journey with "The Secret" did not end there. For two weeks, I re-read the book every day. My ego and Higher-Self entered into battle with each other as doubt and disbelief tried to persuade me from the faith and belief that was slowly returning to me. I was going through some challenges which were weighing heavily on me, so this book came to me at the right time. Talk about the Divine timing!

I decided to put the book to the test; for so long, I had distanced myself from God and stopped asking for help. It was during an O2 exhibition of Doctor Who, during the time David Tennant played the famous doctor.

My son was incredibly excited to see Doctor Who. I had managed to purchase tickets to see the cast of Stargate Atlantis, but to my surprise, I was informed that tickets for Doctor Who had sold out a month earlier. At the gate, this was confirmed to me again. I hadn't the heart to tell my son that there were no tickets left and that he wouldn't be seeing his hero, David Tennant. So, I decided to put the Law of Attraction to the test. I imagined us meeting David Tennant. I willed myself to feel happy and grateful for this opportunity. I believed we would see Doctor Who.

However, upon requesting a couple of tickets at the gate, I was informed there were still no tickets. Nevertheless, I carried on believing. This will happen, I told myself.

At some point, I realised I needed to go to the cashpoint. As I walked to the cashpoint, I suddenly heard footsteps running after me and the staff member who had originally told me there were no tickets left appeared. He informed me that a lady was at the ticket gate and she had a spare Doctor Who ticket because her friend hadn't turned up; she was willing to sell it for half the price.

Overjoyed and thanking the staff member, I pulled the money from the cashpoint and returned to the gate. I purchased the ticket from the lady, and because my son was a minor, I was able to go in with him and see Doctor Who, too!

This was only the beginning of the many remarkable things that have happened since I began to harness the Law of Attraction. Everything started to come together and make sense; I would meet the right people at the right time. This was the beginning of my journey and a new chapter in my life. My faith in God restored, it was time to wake up to my true divinity, and to understand my purpose and fulfil my assignment in this life.

A short time later, I was downloading some audio tapes and came across Doreen Virtue's, "How to Hear Your Angels". At first, I ignored it. However, a nagging voice kept telling me to listen to it. So, I did, and it was then that my understanding of the experiences I'd had throughout my life became clear.

Growing up, I had always known I was different; I could see things other people could not see and hear things others were oblivious to. I would have dreams that would happen, and spirits would appear to me. As a child, I felt confused, lost, and frightened, wondering if I was crazy. It was fantastic, and a significant relief to finally understand my gifts and the purpose of it all. The realisation of the existence of Angels and divinities, it's just extraordinary.

With further studies and research, I came to understand the existence of Angels, Archangels, Guides, Benevolent Entities, and Elementals. My Guides, the Archangels, and years of spiritual studies and self-discovery, have enabled me to understand my true purpose, raise my vibration, and heal myself.

Today, I work as an Angelic Energy Healer, Energy Healer, Angelic channeler, and Medium.

I have simplified this book for the people who are curious and want to connect with these Benevolent Beings. It contains explanations of the Guardian Angels, Spirit Guides, the Archangels, Ascended Masters, Gods and Goddesses that I have worked with. By reading this book, I hope that you will be able to delve a little deeper into the other world, which is all around us, but which we can't necessarily see. You don't have to believe in anything or do anything this book advises; you only need to work with whatever lies in your heart and what your own intuition tells you. This book, which includes descriptions of various Ethereal Beings and Affirmations, is here as a guide and a source of knowledge that will hopefully help you on your spiritual journey as you go through life.

One thing I have learned is that we all possess the courage and strength to manifest the reality we want, no matter who we are. We all have the ability to make life better, both for ourselves and others. Expectations, rules, and regulations which are detrimental to our happiness only hinder the inevitable. We are on a self-discovery and evolutionary soul journey. Thus, by living with all one's heart and soul, believing in the fundamental goodness within, is the first step on the path to happiness, which, in turn, truly helps to make the world a better place. Life is all about learning and evolving.

The affirmations at the end of each "Being" description, teach ways we can invite these Benevolent Beings into our lives to aid and empower us.

Instead of Praying to the Divinities, I have chosen to invoke them by saying: "Thank you for your unconditional love and protection", and using I, or I am, affirmations relating to each Being. The affirmations will connect you to the divinities, and your subconscious mind will start to reprogram itself, shifting the energy and your perspective, thus, raising your vibration.

TABLE OF CONTENTS

ARCHANGEL ARIEL

Archangel Ariel's name means, "Lion, or lioness, of God". Ariel oversees nature, animals, and our own connection to the earthly realm; she is the patron saint of animals and the environment.

Her primary role is to protect, nurture and care for the animals, nature spirit of this earth and all children of Mother Nature. She also assists those who work with the environment and take measures to protect it. The world is in dire strait. Mankind has not fulfilled the duty he was ordained with when he was blessed with overall rule of this world. Many animals are harmed, and much of the land is exploited for our own gain. Ariel helps us to understand, protect the animals and have respect for the environment. She helps explorers and environmentalists who may need protection from the wrath of Mother Nature when they embark on a quest.

Ariel is particularly helpful for those who feel a strong connection with nature and animals.

If you are nursing an animal back to health or campaigning against plastic, or if you are promoting energy-saving ideas or performing magic or rituals among nature, calling on Ariel's guidance can help assist and guide you.

Ariel works particularly closely with Archangel Raphael in healing injured animals and therefore she is wonderfully helpful for vets, rescuers and healers who work closely with animals.

For those who are struggling to make ends meet with regard to basic necessities such as food and water, Ariel can help them climb their way out of this dark place and provide light and shelter where it is needed.

Archangel Ariel helps with:

- Divine magic
- Healing and protecting animals
- Manifestation
- Environmentalism
- Beauty

AFFIRMATION

*Thank You, Archangel Ariel, for Your
unconditional love and protection.
I am a lover of nature and a guardian of
the Earth.
I am strong and bold.
I protect the planet.
I love helping animals, domestic and non-
domestic.
I am brave enough to protect my planet.
I find food and shelter for me and my
family.
I do not fear Nature; we are one and the
same.
The material withers, but the spiritual
lives on.
I help and heal animals.
I respect the land and all who live here.
I believe in the power of trees which are
sacred to me.
I am a warrior of the world who will
defend Mother Nature's children.
I love helping the environment.
I see the beauty in me and in all the
children of Mothers Earth.
I love the planet.*

ARCHANGEL AZRAEL

Archangel Azrael's name means, "Whom God Helps." Azrael is often referred to as the "Angel of Death" because he helps with the transition between life and death, helping those who are crossing over to do so without suffering or pain and help them assimilate on the other side.

Archangel Azrael provides comfort to family and friends during their mourning.

Azrael provides comfort where it is needed and assists the soul in life after leaving the physical body. Losing a loved one triggers immense pain and suffering in many. Azrael calms and assists grieving people and helps to align their mental state in order to deal with the grief.

Death can be a scary and overwhelming time for many. Grief can linger on, long after the loved one has passed. Archangel Azrael provides spiritual counselling and comfort during difficult times. He also guides counsellors' words and actions and shields them from absorbing their client's pain.

The transition between life and death is not easy physically, emotionally, or spiritually. It can be hard to look at the bigger picture of the soul's journey when we are consumed by feelings of loss, sadness, and despair. How can we go on without them? Will we ever heal from this pain? These are all the areas Azrael deals with, assisting and guiding us, and comforting us in our hour of need.

Pain is a part of life, but it does not have to be a negative one. Through pain and transformation, we can reach our soul's purpose. This does not discount the overwhelming love we feel for those who have crossed over; if anything, it highlights just how powerful that love is, for we could not feel such intense emotions of despair without the phenomenal power of love.

Archangel Azrael helps with:

- Comforting the dying and grief-stricken
- Assisting the transition between life and death for the deceased's soul
- Counselling
- Supporting the grieving with mental, spiritual, and emotional help

AFFIRMATION

Thank You, Archangel Azrael, for Your unconditional love and protection.
I am strong and can overcome my grief.
I know that when the body dies, the soul lives on.
My loved one is still with me.
I am grateful for the life I have been given.
I know my loved one will never really leave me.
Death is just the next step in the soul's journey.
I know those who die never truly leave us.
I deal with grief with peace and love in my heart.
I am strong enough to deal with the pain.
My loved ones are at peace and I am at peace.

ARCHANGEL BARACHIEL

Archangel Barachiel's name means, "God's Blessings". We all have Guardian Angels. No soul comes to Earth without the assistance of Guardian Angels who are here to help us as we navigate the twists and turns of life.

Guardian Angels are especially important when we are struggling, or in pain, because it is during these times that their presence is most needed.

Archangel Barachiel is the chief of all Guardian Angels. He is also known as the "Angel of Blessings".

Because Archangel Barachiel's primary role is as chief of the Guardian Angels, it means that he is the one people turn to when they need assistance. Have you noticed how when people are struggling, suffering, or in pain, they will often call out to a higher power to help them? It is Archangel Barachiel who hears the cry for help and filters it down to the other Archangels, as well as to Almighty God Himself.

When you communicate with Barachiel directly, you might experience an extraordinary shift in the way you view things and in the circumstances that unfold.

There is profound, loving energy that he emits, which can be felt profoundly, even if we cannot see him.

I say "Him", but Archangel Barachiel can appear in the form of a male or female because he represents both the Divine Masculine and Divine Feminine. This is why he is also especially helpful to those who are going through the Twin Flame journey, which symbolises pain as much as it symbolises pleasure.

Barachiel is often depicted as scattering rose petals or holding baskets of bread. This is because he is the Archangel of blessings, and his message is a simple one: *You are here to experience the blessings of the world, whether it is through pain or pleasure.* Because Barachiel's messages that pain and pleasure must ultimately come together to experience wholeness, it is believed that those who inspire a strong sense of humour in people who experience blessings through his wisdom. After all, it would be difficult to go through the challenges of life without being able to laugh every now and then!

He is also the patron saint of marriage and families. In astrology, he is linked to Scorpio (the transformation of darkness into light) and Pisces (universal love). His planet affiliation is with Jupiter, the planet of benevolence.

Archangel Barachiel helps with:

- Blessings in family and marriage
- Help in achieving goals
- Achieving blessings through their own personal angels
- Bringing good fortune
- Assisting the Twin Flame relationship

AFFIRMATION

Thank you, Archangel Barachiel, for Your unconstitutional love and protection.

I am a blessing in my life.

I push through adversity.

I see the humour in life.

I succeed in my pursuits.

I contact my Angels and find blessings through them.

I face my Twin Flame relationship.

I am a warrior who never gives up.

I am loved and protected.

I achieve my goals with ease.

ARCHANGEL CASTIEL

Archangel Castiel's name means, "My cover is God", or "Shield of God". Also known as Cassiel, Archangel Castiel is similarly known as the Angel of Temperance. It is his job to bring balance, light where there is dark, to merge the Divine Feminine and the Divine Masculine as one, and to share this knowledge and wisdom with humanity so that we too, can incorporate these fundamental aspects within our being, as one.

Archangel Castiel is a prince of the Seventh Heaven, which is where God sits on his throne. Castiel also has the power to decide who does and who doesn't enter the Seventh Heaven. Because Archangel Castiel's position among the Archangels is of high rank, he is able to watch what happens in the universe without himself interfering.

It is believed that Archangel Castiel also presides over the souls who leave Earth on Judgement Day. When we die, our souls return to the Source from whence we came. It is here that we are given a chance to look back on our lives and see where we went wrong, as well as see the good things we did.

Though it is called Judgement Day, there is no judgement. At least not judgement in the sense that we understand it here on Earth. This judgement enables us as souls to see how we might be able to improve for the next journey.

Archangel Castiel is the ultimate champion of the underdog. Anyone who is sickly, oppressed, in pain, or whose voice and individuality is being stifled, can benefit from Castiel's protection and guidance. It is his job to balance power throughout the world. There must be balance, and that is why Archangel Castiel is also working hard at this moment in time to help balance the world as we shift into the Age of Aquarius, using his blessings and energy to guide us.

He is also associated with the planet Saturn, also known as the Lord of Karma. Saturn is the planet that is known as being the school of hard knocks. The lessons Saturn brings are rarely easy, but they are essential for us to become the best version of ourselves.

With his patience and guidance, Archangel Castiel is the one who teaches us temperance and peace within when the world is crumbling around us. Finding this inner light when in the midst of darkness is the goal of every soul, and Castiel helps us find it.

Archangel Castiel helps with:

- Bringing balance and peace to your inner self
- Easing the souls of the departed into the shadowlands

- Championing the underdog and helping you fight a just cause
- Bringing serenity to the chaos

AFFIRMATION

Thank you, Archangel Castiel, for your unconditional love and protection.

I am protected by Divine Light.

I submit to a Higher Power.

I know the truth within.

I champion for the underdog.

I find peace in the chaos and light in the darkness.

I balance my light and my shadow.

I am wise and knowledgeable.

I am a peace bringer.

ARCHANGEL CHAMUEL

A rchangel Chamuel's name means, "He who sees God", or "he who seeks God."

Archangel Chamuel helps the good vanquish the darkness. He is usually on the list of the seven core Archangels, considered a powerful leader in the angelic hierarchy called 'The Powers'. These 'Powers' are Angels who protect the world from lower energies which instill fear and terror in others. The 'Powers' work as Protectors who shield the world from those who attempt to take over. During the last world war, for example, the 'Powers' assisted Mankind in stopping the rise of Nazi Germany, where millions of people were brutally murdered for their race, religion or creed.

The war between good and evil is an indisputable war that takes place on the earthly realm. But just as the evil is made apparent to us, so is the good. We see good, honest, hardworking people, and also, we see kind, gifted people working as healers to help remove devastation and blocks from people who are suffering.

We see movements growing across the world to help re-balance the earth and make it a better place. Chamuel does not just assist Man on a grand, global scale, but also on an individual one. Where there is fear, darkness, or despair, Chamuel does what he can to enter the hearts of the fearful and lost, providing them with courage and strength to face their adversity.

As well as this, Chamuel is a "finder"- he helps us find items that are lost, and he also helps us to find ourselves. When we feel lost and alone, calling upon Archangel Chamuel's power can help us find who we truly are and set us upon the right path. He helps repair damage both within ourselves and in our relationships. His strength is greatly endorsed by all those seeking to make the world a better place for themselves and those around them.

Archangel Chamuel helps with:

- World peace
- Life purposes
- Strength in the face of adversity
- Careers
- Lost items
- Relationship building and strengthening
- Soul mates

AFFIRMATION

Thank You, Archangel Chamuel, for Your unconditional love and protection.
I am strong.
I am courageous.
I fight against adversity and overcome it.
I defeat the dark forces with love and strength in my heart.
I strive for world peace.
I protect those who are suffering and in pain.
I am a child of God and I find my true path back to him.
I find the career made for me.
I always find my way back to the right path.
I build my relationship with my loved one.
I find my soulmate and become one with each other.
I overcome the challenges in my relationships and seek harmony.
I overcome my fear and anxiety for the greater good.
I am a good person who works for the light and will help drive out the darkness.

ARCHANGEL GABRIEL

Archangel Gabriel's name means, "God is my strength." Archangel Gabriel was mentioned in the Bible as the bringer of messages who, most notably, told the Mother Mary that she would give birth to the baby Jesus. Archangel Gabriel also dictated The Koran to the Prophet Mohammed.

Gabriel is incredibly powerful; she is one of the most powerful in the Angelic Realm and the source of her strength is unlimited. She is able to help countless people simultaneously.

Gabriel works closely with Mankind and is able to communicate with us in the way that is easiest for us to hear her. Whether it is hearing, feeling, seeing or even a sense of smell or taste, Gabriel will work with our easiest channel and reach out to us.

She is one of the Archangels that works with children. Gabriel works to protect children and assists with pregnancy, adoption and birth. Children themselves can sense her presence and love when she is there!

If a child comes to you speaking of a beautiful, winged person with a bright shining light who is encouraging his or her natural playfulness and happiness, don't be so quick to dismiss it as an imaginary friend! It may well be the Archangel Gabriel, loving and protecting the child as she does every single day.

Gabriel is great to work with regarding artists' endeavours, and she assists us with our passion and creativity. When we feel in a slump, dulled, or trapped in the feeling that our innate passion will never be free, calling on Gabriel can help us flourish, removing blockages that hinder us and gently encouraging us to follow our heart's desire.

She protects us and helps us to feel strong and confident, especially when we are feeling weak or suffering from low self-confidence. With Gabriel by our side, there is so much we can achieve.

Like all Archangels, Gabriel first needs to be given permission to help us. This permission must come from ourselves.

Archangel Gabriel helps with:

- Child conception and fertility
- Writing and journalism
- Artists and all related art projects

AFFIRMATION

Thank you, Archangel Gabriel, for Your

unconditional love and protection.

I am creative.

I am passionate.

I harness my passion to its greatest power.

I communicate well with my children.

My children are protected.

I communicate well with those around me.

I am self-confident and powerful.

I am capable of achieving anything I want

to achieve.

I can do anything I set my mind to.

I have great power and self-belief.

I have a brilliant mind that loves to

create.

ARCHANGEL HANIEL

Archangel Haniel's name means, "Glory of God" or "Grace of God". Archangel Haniel helps those who practice in the occult of forms of divination. In the modern era, gifts which are considered 'supernatural' are often seen as suspicious. While such gifts were considered normal centuries ago, especially among ancient civilisations, today's society is dominated by mainstream science, which often scoffs at and dismisses these abilities. Such abilities can range from clairvoyance, mediumship, spiritual healing, astrology, rune reading and many more. For people today who have a natural aptitude for such gifts, it can be hard for them to fit into society and, at times, they may feel like outsiders. This can create feelings of loneliness for the individual.

Archangel Haniel helps to assist and guide those with such powers. In the time of Ancient Babylon, a group of men known as 'priest astronomers', worked with astrology, astronomy, moon energy and various deities for divination and spiritual purposes. One of the Archangels they worked with was Haniel, who was associated with the planet Venus.

Today, people who want to understand and nurture their psychic or mediumship abilities can call on Haniel to help them. It can be especially tough in the modern era because society does not recognise divination as a 'serious' branch.

However, there are still millions of people throughout the world who believe and experience it for themselves; such gifts should never be discounted or downplayed. Haniel helps people understand their gifts so that they may help make life better for themselves, for those around them and for the world at large. It can be frightening, especially at an early age, to see into the spiritual realm or have flashes or visions that come true. But, Haniel can help remove this fear and ease us into understanding our abilities, helping us to master them as we would with any other craft. She can help us have confidence in our gifts and recognise that there was a reason we were given them, and that each and every one of us will, with her guidance and help, discover what those reasons are.

Archangel Haniel helps with:

- Healing abilities
- Moon energy
- Psychic abilities (especially clairvoyance)
- Poise and grace
- Bringing understanding of our abilities into our lives

AFFIRMATION

Thank You, Archangel Haniel, for Your
unconditional love and protection.
I am gifted and I accept all my gifts.
I see things others can't see.
I nurture my unique abilities.
God gave me these gifts to help myself
and people.
There is nothing strange about me; I am
unique and blessed.
I conduct myself with grace and elegance.
I feel the strong pull of the moon and I
use her light to guide me.
I discover my gifts and make the best use
of them.
I am a healer; I heal myself and others.

ARCHANGEL JEHUDIEL

Archangel Jehudiel's name means, "Laudation of God", or "God of the Jews". Archangel Jehudiel is known as the Angel of Work.

Along with Archangel Salaphiel, he presides over the movement of the planets, and this makes him a powerful figure in astrology, assisting those who wish to understand the power and mysteries of the universe.

Archangel Jehudiel assists all those who are looking for work, hoping to change job, feeling defeated by the outcome, suffering confusion due to work and he celebrates the successes of those who are triumphant in their work.

He is incredibly powerful in building people's self-esteem and self-confidence. If you tell yourself you cannot do it, Jehudiel is there to remind you that you can. If you feel overwhelmed or defeated by what is being asked of you, Jehudiel helps to remind you of your inner strength and lets you know that you can overcome any challenge you face.

Archangel Jehudiel helps you see who you are in the eyes of God. This is what truly matters. God loves you, unconditionally. You are beautiful, wise, and magnificent because you are a part of Him. Lack of self-confidence points towards a lack of seeing yourself through God's eyes.

Calling upon Archangel Jehudiel helps you see yourself the same way God sees you and it is through his help that you will be able to see the great light that you truly are.

Jehudiel helps to provide work opportunities for those who wish to be closer to God and the universe. Often, this is done unconsciously and relates to following your soul purpose. If you are going with what you feel in your heart to be true and not caving into the whims or demands around you, you will find it easier to hear the words of your soul.

Jehudiel wants what is best for you and is especially helpful for those who engage in meditation and prayer, who are trying to find their Soul purpose. His kind light and wisdom enable you to remove the clouds that prevent you from seeing the light, and he bestows courage and strength to those who need to break through social norms to follow their true path.

Archangel Jehudiel helps with:

- Prayers related to work
- Finding your soul purpose
- Understanding the working of the planets
- Building self-confidence
- Seeing yourself through the eyes of God
- Providing work opportunities
- Assisting with prayer and meditation

AFFIRMATION

*Thank you, Archangel Jehudiel, for your
unconditional love and protection.
I am a guiding light.
I know my soul purpose.
I manifest the career that I dream of.
I wish to know more about the workings
of the universe
I am a beautiful and wonderful shining
light.
I have the confidence to achieve my
dreams.
I am wonderful just the way I am.
Opportunities abound for me.*

ARCHANGEL JEREMIEL

Archangel Jeremiel's name means, "Mercy of God". Jeremiel represents the most ethereal side of life—what lies beneath the veil of the world we know as opposed to the world we don't. In the ancient Judaic texts, he is listed as one of the seven core Archangels.

Jeremiel relates very much to inner reflection and the core of who we truly are. Often, we can find ourselves on a path in life that does not bring us true fulfilment. For example, we may be in a job that pays extremely well, with a fancy car and luxury house, and yet we can still feel like something is missing from our life. This could very well be because we are unbalanced; we are supposed to have both wealth and spirituality.

Jeremiel is the Archangel of dreams and aspirations. With that being said, this is not what we feel society wants us to achieve, but rather what we feel in our hearts is the right thing to do. We hear of it happening all the time in corporate industries. A successful CEO or manager of a company decides to drop everything to go backpacking across the Andes and explore his or her spiritual side.

This usually happens after some kind of mid-life crisis and intense self-reflection. Jeremiel can help assist with this transition, which can often be painful and befuddling to those around us. For people who are discouraged and troubled, Jeremiel provides hope and encouragement, shedding light where there is darkness or confusion. He is crucial in helping people learn from their mistakes, helping them to realise that their mistake does not necessarily mean failure – rather, it is simply a learning curve, or a stepping stone to become the very best of who we are. Jeremiel helps those who are fighting an inner battle, often between the soul and the ego. This is why his presence is very much of the ethereal world, for this is a battle that takes place between the spiritual and physical planes. Whenever you feel lost, afraid, alone or confused about who you are and what it is you want in life, Jeremiel is there to help you and provide guidance. He also helps assist those who have psychic or prophetic dreams. These can be frightening for someone who has no knowledge of what they entail. Jeremiel helps with understanding these dreams and interpreting them.

Archangel Jeremiel helps with:

- Interpreting psychic dreams
- Life reviewing
- Making changes in life
- Understanding the internal battle between soul and ego

AFFIRMATION

*Thank You, Archangel Jeremiel, for Your
unconditional love and protection.
When I am lost, the way is shown to me.
I find my true path.
I understand my dreams and how they can
help me find clarity.
I move past my troubles and find my
purpose.
I love venturing into the unknown.
I am brave and I face everything with love
and strength.
I am genuinely happy.
I move forward positively with my destiny.
I have great gifts.
My path to enlightenment is clear.
It is easy for me to make decisions.
I am wise and capable.*

ARCHANGEL JOPHIEL

Archangel Jophiel's name means, "Beauty of God" and she is known as the patron of artists.

Archangel Jophiel is helpful for all artists and creative types. It was Jophiel who was present in the Garden of Eden and helped Adam and Eve appreciate the beauty of the garden; later, she appeared again to watch over the sons of Noah, Ham, Shem, and Japheth.

Creativity is something crucial to our world, and yet its importance is often downplayed in modern society. For all the flaws of this world, there are many virtues also and true art is the understanding that light and dark must be united in order to reach a state of true equilibrium.

The artistic mind understands this fully in their subconscious. To a degree, all of us are artists, but some express it more readily than others. Art is merely the soul's way of expressing itself. Call on Jophiel when you are needing inspiration and to see the beauty of this life.

It can be hard to see beauty when things appear cruel, hard, and despairing, but Jophiel reminds us that even in the deepest, darkest corners, beauty can still be found, whether it is outside of us or inside us.

As the Archangel of both art and beauty, Jophiel helps us both physically and metaphysically. She helps us to think beautiful thoughts, dissipating negativity when it overpowers our minds. She helps us to see and appreciate the beauty all around us; by doing so, she is able to help us attract and manifest beauty into our own lives. She helps us create beauty in our homes and environment.

Jophiel helps those with low self-esteem and lack of self-confidence recognise their own beauty, gently guiding them toward self-love and empowerment. When we feel that the world is an ugly place or that others are exhibiting ugliness through cruelty, selfishness or hatred, calling upon Jophiel reminds us of the great good that exists in this world, helping to shed light where there is darkness and beauty where there is despair.

Archangel Jophiel helps with:

- Assisting and guiding artists
- Seeing the beauty of life and in others
- Providing us with beautiful thoughts
- Interior decorating
- Slowing down when the pace of life becomes too fast

AFFIRMATION

*Thank You, Archangel Jophiel, for Your
unconditional love and protection.
I am beautiful.
The world is beautiful.
There is much kindness and beauty in
life.
I make my home beautiful.
I create wonderful pieces of art.
I use art to inspire others.
I use my talent to make the world a better
place.
I take time to appreciate the beauty
around me.
I allow myself to think beautiful thoughts.
I release negativity.
I am empowered.
I focus on the light, not the darkness.
I play my role to bring beauty to this
world.*

ARCHANGEL METATRON

Unlike many of the Archangels, the meaning of Archangel Metatron's name is not clear. This is because his name doesn't end in the 'el' suffix, as with the other Archangels. The other exception to the rule is Metatron's twin brother, Sandalphon, who was the Prophet Elijah.

The uniqueness of Metatron's name likely stems from his unusual origins. Along with Archangel Sandalphon, he was the only other Archangel to walk the earth as a mortal man. When Metatron was human, he was the skilled and honest scribe, Enoch. After Enoch's death, he ascended into Heaven with wings bestowed upon him. As a scribe on Earth, Enoch was given a similar job in Heaven. He is the one who had to record everything that happened on Earth and keep it in the Akashic Records, otherwise known as the Book of Life.

Archangel Metatron is the patron of scribe-keeping, writing and organisation. He is especially helpful for those who have busy schedules or whose hectic lifestyles can be hard to juggle at times.

Metatron helps us become more organized, subsequently reducing stress levels. He is especially helpful for busy mothers who must juggle work, family and household chores all at once! He is also a wonderful aide for writers and authors, especially those struggling with writer's block, helping them to remove any blockages and tap into their creativity.

Metatron is wonderful for helping children, especially those with Attention Deficit Disorder (ADD) or Attention Deficit Hyperactivity Disorder (ADHD). He helps to support families and friends who may sometimes struggle in this area as he provides clarity, wisdom and understanding.

Metatron is especially good for helping people understand their spiritual side. It can be hard for us to delve deep into our spiritual aspects in a world dominated by the physical and material, but as C.S Lewis said: "You do not have a soul. You are a soul. You have a body." Metatron helps people to understand how to use their spiritual side for its intended purpose — for the good of themselves, others, and the world at large. Once such understanding is made clear to the individual, suddenly physical and material gain mean truly little and a deep desire to spread compassion and one's own individual talents come into play. Also, Metatron is great for time warping. When you are late or stuck in traffic, ask Metatron to help you get there on time.

Archangel Metatron helps with:

- Children's issues such as ADD and ADHD
- Record-keeping and organisation

- Spiritual understanding
- Writing
- Time Warping

AFFIRMATION

Thank You, Archangel Metatron, for
Your unconditional love and protection.
I understand my children's individual
issues and help them understand.
I am patient with any problems my child
has.
As a teacher, I help children who need
extra help in areas of learning.
I conquer my writer's block.
I am a creative force and I tell wonderful
stories.
I manage my time-keeping better.
I am organised and functional.
I get things done without descending into
stress.
I discover my spiritual side.
I use my spiritual gifts to help others.
I use my spiritual gifts to help myself.
I am a spiritual being learning to use my
talents to make the world better.

ARCHANGEL MICHAEL

Archangel Michael's name means, "He who is like God". Archangel Michael is a leader among the Archangels.

He is in charge of the order of angels known as "the Virtues", and he oversees the lightworker's life purpose.

Michael is extremely tall and handsome, and he usually carries a sword, which he uses to release us from the snare of fear. When he's around, you may see sparkles or flashes of bright blue or purple light. Michael is a fiery energy, and his presence is enough to make you sweat.

Michael's light not only overpowers the darkness, but drives the darkness into the light, pushing it out from the shadows and exposing it for all to see. Very often, the darkness can only be defeated when it is pushed into the open; it thrives most when it is hidden. Those on earth who live to do the right thing, who are brave, compassionate, kind and loving, will very often face some of the most distressing and difficult challenges.

This is because the dark forces know which side they are working for and they will do everything to stop them.

This is when the power of Michael reaches down to protect and defend us.

No matter what we are facing and no matter how grave our troubles may be, if we call upon Michael, he will listen. He will protect us, defend us and encourage us not to give up. He is the courageous spirit of fortitude and he will give us this spirit if we should only ask for it.

We all feel alone sometimes; we feel helpless or feel like giving up and we want to retreat into a shell and hide away from all that is dark and evil in this world. Michael is there to remind us that the light will always overpower the darkness. The darkness can never win because the light has love on its side – and there is no force on earth more powerful than the power of love.

When we need reassurance in our own strength and ability, we need to call on Michael and ask for his help. Let his light and strength into your heart.

Archangel Michael helps with:

- Commitment
- Dedication
- Courage
- Direction
- Motivation
- Protection
- Space clearing
- Spirit releasement
- Life's purpose
- Increased self-confidence

AFFIRMATION

Thank You, Archangel Michael, for Your
unconditional love and protection.
I am strong.
I am a warrior.
I face my fears head on.
I bring light to myself and to the world.
I remove doubt and insecurity from my
life.
I am courageous.
I am protected.
I am confident.
I stand in my power.
I am motivated.
I have direction in my life.
I clear my space from negative energy.
I am committed to myself and my work.

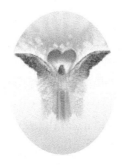

ARCHANGEL NATHANIEL

Archangel Nathaniel's name means, "God has given" or "Gift of God". Nathaniel is the Archangel of life purpose, transformation, manifestation, fire, energy, passion, and purification. It is said that he arrived in 2012 when Mankind began the shift toward the Golden Age and that he has been here ever since, guiding us with passion and energy through our ascendance and transformation.

Some people have felt the shift stronger than others. Some are "waking up." This is part of the divine plan which will help the human race become the best of itself, where compassion and empathy take precedence over the material structure which has dominated this world for millennia. Archangel Nathaniel is an integral part of this shift. He holds ultimate dominion over fire energy, the element that is responsible for action, change and drive. He motivates change for the higher good and pushes us to move forward and blossom, like the caterpillar that becomes a butterfly.

Procrastination is no longer a problem when Nathaniel is around. He embellishes the 'I Am that I Am' inside of us, helping us to understand our true potential and worth.

He cuts through self-doubt and low self-esteem, guiding us in making changes to things that we didn't even realise were problems. Through his love and wisdom, we recognise that we are all part of the same source and one of our fundamental life lessons is to wake up to our own power and utilise the extraordinary abilities we each possess.

If confusion about where you are heading in life is a daily occurrence, or passion has left your life, or things have become dull or stagnant, call on Nathaniel to help you realise who you truly are. Feeling lost is common among us here on Earth. There is no one who has not felt lost and afraid, regardless of the frequency of this feeling. Nathaniel can help show us the way. The process can be long and challenging for some, but each day brings a new life lesson. We are here for a reason and a purpose. Nathaniel shines a light to help us find this purpose, lending us his own divine strength and willpower so we may be bold and brilliant enough to go out into the world and show them exactly what we are made of.

Archangel Nathaniel helps with:

- Transformation
- Manifestation
- Ascension
- Waking up to our own strengths and abilities
- Finding our own sense of worth
- Understanding our transformation as a collective species and in the wider world
- Procrastination

- Eliminating lethargy and dullness in one's life
- Finding a sense of direction and purpose
- Motivation

AFFIRMATION

*Thank You, Archangel Nathaniel, for
Your unconditional love and protection.
I become the best of myself.
I assist this world in being the best of
itself.
I help others be the best of themselves.
I am strong and powerful.
I have special abilities and I use them.
I am worthy and honest.
I am important to this world.
I get up and do things.
I am free of procrastination.
I have excitement and joy in my life.
I do what I am meant to do.
I am the brightest version of myself.
I am motivated and driven.
I achieve anything I put my mind to.
I find direction and purpose.
I help others find direction and purpose.
I am motivated.
I manifest the things I want to rapidly.*

ARCHANGEL ORION

Archangel Orion's name represents a constellation of the three brightest stars known as Orion's Belt or the Belt of Orion, and it is through this constellation that Orion manifests his healing throughout the earth.

Archangel Orion- the Angel of manifestation! This is one of the most magical and powerful Archangels. We are in a time of great change and upheaval. The world is slowly shifting from the Age of Pisces into the Age of Aquarius. The Age of Pisces brought with it hierarchy and the understanding of universal love. The Age of Aquarius now brings equality, individuality, and an application of this love to the physical realm. But this type of transition is never easy, and this is what Archangel Orion helps us with. There is not one of us who is not being affected by this shift, and we are feeling it on both an individual and global level. Orion especially helps those with spiritual gifts, such as clairvoyance, clairsentience, and other abilities, enabling them to develop them in harmony and without interference.

Archangel Orion also offers protection from dark forces and negative entities.

Where these exist in your life, calling upon Orion can help you be rid of them and remove them, so they no longer plague you.

One of the things that Orion is especially known for is the power of manifestation. Manifestation is where you bring your thoughts into reality. You send a message to the universe that you want something to happen – and happen it does! Calling upon Orion to help you manifest enables you to understand manifestation more easily and also gives you added insight into how to manifest at the most potent level.

Archangel Orion is not just about the magic, however. He is also excellent in offering practical advice which helps with all kinds of earthly matters. Generally, Orion has light-hearted, upbeat, and positive energy, and he can help bring good vibes to any situation you find yourself in. This is why his energy is particularly important at the moment. Uncertainty and fear are rife, and it is here that Orion can bestow his light, healing, wisdom, and guidance.

This is one of the most magical Archangel to work with. Therefore, he also brings guidance and assistance to those that practice magic and wish to explore their magical abilities further.

Archangel Orion helps with:

- Manifestation
- Protection from dark forces
- Assistance in the practice of magic
- Help with practical issues

- Bringing positive energy to negative situations
- Assistance and guidance for those with spiritual gifts

AFFIRMATION

Thank you, Archangel Orion, for your

unconventional love and protection.

I am guided and healed by your light.

I am gifted and powerful.

I am protected from dark forces.

I can see the positive in the negative.

I use my magic for good.

I can face any challenge in the physical

world that comes my way.

I am loved and protected.

I manifest what I want effortlessly.

ARCHANGEL RAGUEL

Archangel Raguel's name means, "Friend of God". He is the Archangel of peace and harmony. His primary role in Heaven is to oversee all the other Archangels and angels. He ensures that they are all working together in an orderly and harmonious fashion, in accordance with Divine Order and Will.

Raguel's talents for peace and harmony are not just exclusive to the angelic realm. He helps us here on Earth, too. Human relationships are an essential part of our being. We can love and hate in equal measure. Relationships can cause us great joy or great pain. Love and pain are often closely intertwined, and as we grow as humans, we discover ways to deal with our relationships that can be beneficial to ourselves and our loved ones.

Archangel Raguel helps us learn cooperation, peace, and harmony with our loved ones. He helps smooth over conflicts or disagreements which can lead to stony silence for many years or raging arguments that can have devastating outcomes for all involved.

He promotes peace, understanding and empathy, as well as the knowledge that those we love do love us just as much and all we need to do is acquire an innate understanding of this to improve our relationships.

Raguel is a great defender of the underdog, helping promote courage within us to stand up for those who cannot speak for themselves. Children, the elderly and animals are all examples of the types of beings Raguel encourages us to defend, particularly when they are subjected to tyranny of any kind. He also urges us to stand up for ourselves if we are being treated badly at home, work or within social situations.

Calling upon the courage and understanding of Raguel helps us to stand up against our oppressors and therefore he is a wonderful Archangel for movements or campaigns which challenge those in power who are abusing their position and failing to use such authority for its intended purpose: the good of mankind and all the inhabitants of this world. He helps bring law and order back to chaotic situations and promotes a sense of calm and peace, washing away the ego in favour of the giving and loving soul. When you need courage to stand by the strength of your convictions and the wisdom to see things from others 'points of view', call on Archangel Raguel to guide and assist you in your journey.

Archangel Raguel helps with:

- Resolving arguments
- Harmony and cooperation in families and groups
- Defending the unfairly treated

- Empowerment of self, especially for the underdog
- Mediation of disputes
- Orderliness

AFFIRMATION

*Thank You, Archangel Raguel, for Your
unconditional love and protection.
I love and care for my loved ones and I
try to understand them.
I forgive others who have hurt me.
I forgive myself for hurting others.
I work with those around me with peace
and harmony.
I keep things peaceful for myself and
others.
I defend the underdog.
I fight for those who can't speak for
themselves.
I have the courage of my convictions.
I have the wisdom to see all points of
view.
I come to a peaceful arrangement for the
good of all.
I am motivated by empathy and peace.
I strive for order among the chaos.
I help those around me to be more
empathic and harmonious.
I am a peace bringer and a peacemaker.
I am peaceful and harmonious.*

ARCHANGEL RAPHAEL

Archangel Raphael's name means, "God heals", or, "God healed". Archangel Raphael is one of the more famous and widely known among the Archangels. Archangel Raphael's abilities revolve very much around the aspect of healing.

If you, or someone you know, is feeling sickly or poor, whether physically, mentally, emotionally, or spiritually, then Raphael is the one to call on. He is a powerful healer. Raphael will go wherever is requested of him and aid whoever is suffering. However, he cannot interfere with a person's free will; ultimately, it's up to the individual if they accept the healing, so it's best to seek that person's permission first.

Raphael does not just heal humans, but animals also, and he helps find them when they are lost. All of God's creatures will benefit from his powerful healing abilities.

Raphael's presence is extremely soothing and comforting. He is wonderful in helping to wash away fears and anxieties.

For those who suffer from anxiety, stress, insomnia (induced by racing, unwanted thoughts) or constant worries, Raphael heals naturally and gradually, helping to bring clarity to a weary mind and slowly driving the sufferer into a place of peace. He helps those who are struggling with addictions and cravings, helping to reduce the urge for them or eliminating them entirely. Such addictions can have an enormous strain on both the individual and those around them, and Raphael helps to soothe the anxious minds of loved ones while helping the individual conquer such addictions.

Archangel Raphael also helps with clairvoyance and psychic abilities, helping the individual tap into their higher self. He is also very good at helping spirits trapped on earth move forward and clearing negative energy in people's homes. Overall, Raphael is a multi-dimensional Archangel with a wide array of talents.

He helps keep travellers safe while exploring and he's great to work with for opening your third eye.

Archangel Raphael helps with:

- Healing people and animals
- Providing support and guidance to healers
- Addictions and cravings
- Clairvoyance
- Physical and spiritual eyesight (opening the Third Eye)
- Finding lost pets
- Space clearing

- Spirit release
- Protecting travellers and bringing harmony on their journeys

AFFIRMATION

Thank You, Archangel Raphael, for Your

unconditional love and protection.

I heal myself and others.

I am worthy of healing.

I heal to become the best of myself.

I beat my addiction and cravings.

I conquer my cravings.

I develop my psychic abilities.

I open my third eye.

My space is a place of peace.

My home is harmonious.

I am protected on my travels.

I have harmony and order on my travels.

I am a powerful healer.

I am healed.

I am profoundly clairvoyant.

ARCHANGEL RAZIEL

Archangel Raziel's name means, "Secret of God". Archangel Raziel is the Archangel of mystics, clairvoyance and psychic abilities and He knows all of the secrets of the universe and how it operates.

The physical world, the one we are most familiar with, can sometimes block us from exploring the 'other side'. Everyone has psychic abilities to a degree, but some are undoubtedly more powerful than others. As a society, we are taught to oppress such gifts; people with these abilities are often labelled as 'weird 'or 'outcasts '- something no one likes to hear about themselves.

But, for many, as time goes on, they learn to embrace their gifts. Clairvoyants, Alchemists, Magicians, Witches, Clairsentients – these people, and people with these gifts, who are so often shunned by society, find meaning for them and learn to appreciate the abilities they were given.

Raziel helps these gifted individuals find their true path and enhance their abilities. He helps them learn how to master them, so they do not become out of control.

He helps them find purpose so they may be used for the greater good of all.

He also helps provide clarity and wisdom so that the individual understands why they were granted these powers and what they are to be used for.

Raziel helps in understanding esoteric material, manifestation principles, sacred geometry, quantum physics and other high-level information. Slowly but surely, the world is transcending and these studies are taking a very real place in the world of education and society. Raziel not only assists individuals with these topics, but also all of Mankind, helping to ease them into this transition and broadening their minds.

It can be frightening exploring this side of life. Often, people are caught up in the immediate world, the physical one, which consists purely of jobs, money, physical relationships, physical bodies, things and the acquirement of things. Veering too much in this direction can be detrimental to overall growth and well-being. Calling on Raziel can help bring balance between the physical and spiritual world, simultaneously easing this world into a state of equilibrium.

Archangel Raziel helps with:

- Alchemy
- Clairvoyance
- Divine Magic
- Esoteric Information
- Manifestation
- Psychic Abilities

AFFIRMATION

Thank You, Archangel Raziel, for Your
unconditional love and protection.
I understand my abilities and make the
most of them.
I am gifted.
I welcome all of my gifts.
I am unique, individual, and powerful.
I know there are others like me.
I am different to others but that is OK.
I manifest anything I want.
I use my gifts for the greater good.
I control my abilities.
I am whoever I want to be.
I make this world however I want it to be.
I help others with their gifts.
I believe in the great power within me.
I am an alchemist.
I am profoundly clairvoyant.
I am grateful and I love my psychic
abilities.

ARCHANGEL REMIEL

Archangel Remiel name means, "Mercy of God". Archangel Remiel is one of the seven Archangels who stands close by God's side. He is also known as the Angel of Hope.

Archangel Remiel has several vital roles among the Archangels, and he is especially helpful to those who are struggling with negative thoughts, depression, or sadness.

It is Remiel that God sends to those who are experiencing difficulty. Remiel brings light where there is darkness and encourages you to never give up.

When swamped in dark clouds, it can be hard to reach out at all. However, if you can find it within yourself to call Archangel Remiel, he will answer, and light will find its way into your life.

Remiel is also strongly associated with the dead. He guides souls into heaven once their physical body has died.

His nurturing and kind presence enables all those who are suffering to find hope where there is sorrow.

Astrologically, he can be most associated with the signs Pisces and Sagittarius. Sagittarius, the sign of optimism, and Pisces, the sign of unconditional love and compassion. Archangel Remiel has a positive and uplifting energy which can send away even the darkest clouds.

Remiel also has the potential to help us change our lives for the better. Calling upon his help and wisdom means accepting change into your life. He is a powerful Archangel to help those who suffer from mental illness and addictions, as he helps to provide the strength and courage to help them get better.

This Archangel sees the negativity of the world and seeks to bring light to it. Therefore, those who are also concerned about world events and the suffering of others can also call upon Remiel to shed his light on them. He is the one Archangel who can offer help on a grand scale and protect those who needs protection the most. If there is someone in the public eye or on a global scale you want to protect, then calling Archangel Remiel to surround them with light is a wonderful way to harness his powerful energy.

Archangel Remiel helps with:

- Helping those who are sad and depressed
- Helping those with mental illness or addiction
- Protecting public figures and people who are distant from you
- Instigating positive change in our lives
- Guiding souls into heaven

AFFIRMATION

Thank you, Archangel Remiel, for your
unconditional love and protection.
I overcome and heal my depression.
I overcome my sadness.
I transform my life for the better.
I overcome and heal my addiction.
I pray for the souls of the departed.
I protect those who need it most.
My loved ones are protected.
I am loved and protected.

ARCHANGEL SANDALPHON

A rchangel Sandalphon is one of two archangels whose name doesn't end in' el'. Sandalphon means' brother' in Greek and is a reference to his twin brother, Archangel Metatron. Metatron and Sandalphon are the only archangels from Heaven who were originally mortal men before God transformed them into Archangels. Metatron was the wise man, Enoch, while Sandalphon was the prophet, Elijah.

Archangel Sandalphon has specific missions in helping mankind. He is responsible for delivering people's prayers to God and he also orchestrates the music in Heaven. When we hear beautiful music that reminds us of a time and place we struggle to remember, very often it is Archangel Sandalphon guiding this music to our ears so that we may feel closer to the heavenly realm. When we pray and ask that God hears our call, it is Archangel Sandalphon who delivers our message to the higher realm, bringing forth a greater connection between us and the Almighty.

Because Sandalphon was a mortal, he has been accorded the duty of inspiring mankind to take better care of the earth. All around us, we can see the devastation that has been wrought because of our actions.

Famine, war, the destruction of nature and the abuse towards our fellow species and animals are all examples of this. Sandalphon encourages us to use our innate compassion and wisdom to help heal this world. He is wonderful in aiding those who are seeking purpose and trying to discover what their role on earth is. He helps us reconnect with nature and remind ourselves that we are all at one with each other – people, animals, plants and minerals. Because we are all connected through one essence – the Universe and God – Archangel Sandalphon encourages us to care for others as we would care for ourselves. By doing so, he helps raise us to a higher consciousness where we prioritise the well-being of others and our planet over everyone else.

Archangel Sandalphon assists all those who wish to connect to God. This does not have to be in the form of any organised religion or through any set of rules. Anyone can connect to God and the universe and it is the essential right of their soul to do so. Whatever way one may pray, whether through traditional prayer, simply closing one's eyes or engaging in rituals, Archangel Sandalphon helps our message reach God. He reminds us that we are all children of God, no matter who we are or what our beliefs are.

Archangel Sandalphon helps with:

- Music
- Delivering and answering prayers
- Determining the gender of unborn babies

AFFIRMATION

Thank You, Archangel Sandalphon, for
Your unconditional love and protection.
I speak to God and I am heard.
I hear the messages sent to me from
heaven.
I am a child of God and the universe.
Music helps my life become more
beautiful and peaceful.
The music of heaven is the music of
Earth.
I believe that earth and heaven are
connected.
I am a guardian of the planet and will
assist it.
I am a healer of this world and People.
I believe we are all connected as one.
I love this world and I use my gifts to
help it.
I am a source of light in this world.
I know my child's gender before they
arrive on earth.

ARCHANGEL SARIEL

Archangel Sariel's name means, "Prince of God", or, "God's Prince". Archangel Sariel is of the most powerful and just like Archangel Samsiel, he is one of the angels that fell to earth. This makes him a holy angel and a fallen angel. Thus, like Archangel Samsiel, he has experience and knowledge of the dark human side of life.

Just as one of Archangel Samsiel's roles was to teach people about magic and encourage occult practitioners to harness their natural abilities, one of Archangel Sariel's key roles is to teach about the phases of the Moon. Therefore, he is an excellent archangel to call upon for those interested in studying the Moon and understanding how Moonology can lead to manifestation, which can help improve their lives and the lives of others.

Astrologically, Archangel Sariel is associated with the sign of Aries, which is ruled by Mars, the planet of war. Aries is a fire sign which is known for its courage and strength of conviction. The sign of Aries understands the fires of war and accepts that life is not all sunshine and roses.

Archangel Sariel is also known as the 'Angel of Punishment and Death.' Sariel is the one known for punishing sin and evil inflicted on others. As Archangel Sariel is a warrior angel, he is also able to offer protection from malevolent forces and those who wish to do you harm. But as well as being a warrior, he is also an angel of healing. Therefore, he is a powerful ally for those who fight the dark forces and who are targets for malevolent entities. Archangel Sariel offers strength and protection, as well as healing for those who are wounded in their battle against the dark forces.

Another powerful way Sariel can help you is when the universe and God are directing you to your life purpose, and significant upheaval occurs. This is especially true for those who experience a 'mid-life crisis', and everything seems to suddenly spiral out of control. Calling upon Archangel Sariel for help during times of upheaval helps bring inner stability to you and faith that everything is in Divine Order. God has a plan for you, and Sariel helps to remind you of your soul mission.

Additionally, Archangel Sariel helps those who are feeling overwhelmed or anxious due to challenging situations and experiences. Calling on his wisdom and guidance can help reduce stress and ease tension.

Archangel Sariel helps with:

- Understanding Moon manifestation
- Protection from dark forces
- Understanding crisis and your life purpose

- Recognizing the Divine Order
- Anxiety and stress
- Healing

AFFIRMATION

Thank you, Archangel Sariel, for your

unconditional love and protection.

I am strong.

I defeat the dark forces.

I am a warrior of the light.

I harness the energy of the Moon to

manifest my reality.

I surrender to the Divine Order and my

life purpose.

I conquer anxiety.

I am guided and protected.

I am healed.

ARCHANGEL SELAPHIEL

Archangel Selaphiel's name means, "The Prayer of God". Archangel Selaphiel is one who connects the prayers of mankind to God.

Selaphiel has a gentle and loving energy that eclipses fear, anxiety, and doubt. Praying to God may seem like a simple task to some, but it is more complicated than that. Sometimes, negative thoughts overshadow the message one wants to get across from within their soul. Archangel Selaphiel helps to dispel these fears so that our desires and needs are heard loudly and clearly.

Selaphiel is also extremely helpful to those who wish to interpret their dreams. Calling upon him after you have had a confusing or intense dream can help you understand it better. Either you will receive a clear message or a symbolic one.

Selaphiel helps those struggling and suffering from addiction, helping to bring strength and clarity to them. For those who wish to pray for an addict, he helps bring them soothing and calm, easing their fears and distress. Selaphiel is also a protector of children and listens to the prayers of children, carrying them to God.

One of the beautiful aspects of Archangel Selaphiel is that he rules over the music in heaven and leads the heavenly choir. He is also excellent help to those who have a musical voice on earth, helping them to nurture their talent and push through shyness or self-doubt that may be holding them back.

Archangel Selaphiel's loving light presides over the exorcisms on Earth. He helps to cast out demons and bring courage to those who are suffering from them. He hears and answers the prayers of those who pray to God for a loved one who is suffering from demonic influence or negative entities that have found their way to a human body or environment. He is especially helpful to exorcists and priests.

In astrology, he is known as the Angel of the Sun, and along with Archangel Jehudiel rules the movement of planets.

Archangel Selaphiel helps with:

- Carrying prayers to God
- Dispelling fear
- Those suffering from addiction
- Protecting children
- Guiding the musically gifted
- Understanding astrology
- Assisting with exorcisms and getting rid of negative entities
- Dream interpretation

AFFIRMATION

Thank you, Archangel Selaphiel, for your
unconditional love and protection.
I am loved and protected.
My prayers are being heard.
I am calm and loved.
I overcome my addiction.
My loved one overcome their addiction.
I protect my children.
I am talented and use my talent for its
intended purpose.
I understand the working of the planets.
My dreams have meaning and will help.
guide me.
I cast out negative entities.

ARCHANGEL SHAMSIEL

Archangel Shamsiel name means, "Mighty God of Sun". Archangel Shamsiel is one who appears as both a fallen angel and a holy one. He assisted Uriel in battle.

Shamsiel is one of the highest-ranking of the archangels, residing in the fourth heaven with Archangel Michael and Archangel Sandalphon. One of his most important tasks for humanity is to take our prayers to the fifth heaven, where God receives them and where the power of manifestation resides.

The interesting thing about Archangel Shamsiel is that he also fell to earth, hence also being known as a 'fallen angel'. It is believed he was one of the angels that rebelled against God and taught the world about war and magic. He also taught about the 'Signs of the Sun', teaching humanity about astrology and being able to read a person's natal chart, fortune, and destiny, as well as the fate of humanity. Therefore, Shamsiel is especially helpful to those who practice the occult: magicians, witches, wiccans, shamans, and astrologers.

All others who have an interest in this area may be able to benefit from Shamsiel's vast wisdom by reaching out to him.

Some believe that communicating directly with Archangel Shamsiel is not a good idea because he fell from Heaven. But he is one of the highest-ranking archangels who rule over the fourth heaven and has a significant role to play among God's army. Archangel Shamsiel can be likened to *Solomon Kane,* who started bad, became good, and then used the knowledge he learned while being bad to fight the darkness for the good. The knowledge and wisdom he imparted on the world in regard to war and magic can be used for great good, just as it can be used for great evil. Therefore, Shamsiel's story is an important one. It shows that to find an effective way to battle the darkness; one must first go through the darkness themselves – for how else are we meant to learn how to defeat our enemy, without exploring every aspect of their strategy and how they think and fight?

Shamsiel can also be likened to the sign of Scorpio in astrology, which is also represented by the *Ray of Harmony Through Conflict.* This is the sign that must confront the darkness within in order to find the light. Scorpio is also the ruler of the 8th house, which is the house of the occult.

Archangel Shamsiel helps with:

- Delivering messages to the fifth heaven
- Helping those involved in conflict
- Enabling us to see the light among the dark

- Enabling us to view what lies beneath, disregarding superficial or shallow appearances
- Bringing greater knowledge to occult practitioners

AFFIRMATION

Thank you, Archangel Shamsiel, for your
unconditional love and protection.
I am guided and supported.
I am strong and brave.
I am gifted in magic.
I am able to go through the darkness to
reach the light.
I can see beneath the surface and beyond
the lies.
I have wisdom of the dark side of life and
will use it for the greater good.
I am love and light.

ARCHANGEL URIEL

Archangel Uriel's name means, "God is light", or, "Fire of God". Uriel's name is befitting for he represents wisdom in all its elements, the light at the end of the tunnel or the light shining in the darkness. Sometimes, when confusion and feelings of being lost consume us, we can feel as if a heavy darkness is settling upon us. But every now and then, a chink of light appears to provide wisdom and guidance. This is Archangel Uriel's purpose and his shining wisdom seeps throughout the whole of mankind so we may make informed choices and find practical solutions for the benefit of ourselves and humanity.

Decision-making is a difficult process at times, both on an individual and collective level. How many times have we agonised over which road to take, wondering if we are making the right decision? How many times have governments, or organisations, decided something which has had a detrimental effect on humanity as a whole?

No one knows what the future holds, but by enlisting the help of Uriel, we can do our best to make decisions that will be for the positive, not the negative. Uriel helps us tap into our own soul's wisdom – the wisdom of God.

Destructive emotions are also something Uriel helps with. When we are clouded by anger, pride, judgement or any other emotion that blocks us from seeing things clearly, we are more likely to make decisions that hinder our progress. Uriel helps people let go of such emotions so that we may move forward with greater clarity.

Uriel greatly helps those who seek greater intellectual information and creative pursuits. He is much revered in the area of arts and he can help people tap into their creativity, mingling divine wisdom with creative manifestation. He is very helpful to writers, especially those with writer's block, and he also helps with the weather. Call out to Uriel asking for good weather on a day you must do something outdoors and he will answer your call! Uriel also helps with natural disasters, aiding those caught in its midst and providing protection wherever possible.

Archangel Uriel helps with:

- Alchemy
- Divine magic
- Earth changes
- Problem solving
- Spiritual understanding
- Studies
- Students and exams
- Weather and writing

AFFIRMATION

*Thank You, Archangel Uriel, for Your
unconditional love and protection.
I find wisdom even when I am confused.
Wisdom is there for me if I need it.
I find light in the darkness.
I control my negative emotions and see
clearly.
I let go of negativity and move into
positive thinking.
I am intellectual and I seek greater
wisdom for it.
I am a creative force.
I overcome my writer's blocks.
I use the power of divine magic for the
greater good.
I solve all problems I am faced with.
I have a greater understanding of the
spirit world.
I succeed in my exams and aspirations.
I use the power of my mind to manifest
anything I choose.
I am an Alchemist.
I understand my spirituality.*

ARCHANGEL ZADKIEL

Archangel Zadkiel's name means, "The righteousness of God", or, "He of Mercy". This title often brings sighs of relief and even silent moments of praise when the name appears. In a world rife with judgement, hardship, mistakes, coldness, and an absence of forgiveness—particularly collectively—Archangel Zadkiel is one of the most important angels in terms of compassion and forgiveness. He is considered both on the Angelic and Earthly realms to be the Archangel of mercy and benevolence.

How many times have we done something that we feel unable to forgive ourselves for? How many times has someone hurt us and we have found it challenging, if not impossible, to forgive them? Have we allowed guilt to swallow us whole or bitterness to consume us? Being unable to forgive oneself or others can lead to a closed heart, which in turn leads to a colder world. Only by accepting and forgiving can we begin the journey to healing; Zadkiel is an integral part of that journey.

We need only ask for his help and he will be more than willing to guide and assist us. Feelings of entrapment and loss that come when we feel betrayed, or when we have betrayed ourselves, are natural and it is important we accept these emotions; to bury or ignore them is to allow them to fester. Zadkiel can help us move forward, encouraging forgiveness and mercy while helping us to understand that each and every person is on their own separate journey.

He helps us understand that making mistakes is a fundamental part of life, and that even those who hurt us willingly are worthy of forgiveness, for we are all part of the same divine light that exists in the universe. Zadkiel can act as a chimney sweeper who cleans your mind, body, and heart, removing the debris of bitterness, resentment, or guilt.

He is also wonderful in helping us to remember things or finding things that are lost. He is particularly helpful for students who need to remember important information for their tests and exams.

Calling upon Zadkiel can greatly assist us as human beings, particularly in the very delicate realm of forgiveness and mercy.

Archangel Zadkiel helps with:

- Compassion
- Forgiveness of self and others
- Emotional and physical healing
- Memory enhancement
- Remembering important information

- Studies, students, and tests
- Finding lost objects

AFFIRMATION

Thank You, Archangel Zadkiel, for Your
unconditional love and protection.
I forgive myself.
I forgive others for hurting me.
I forgive the world.
I let go of my past and forgive any
wrongdoing.
I believe in mercy and compassion.
I heal and let go of any past hurts.
I forgive those who have done wrong.
I forgive myself for doing wrong.
I am on a journey of forgiveness and
enlightenment.
I remember important information.
I succeed in my studies.
I find the things I have lost.
I improve and enhance my memory.

ARCHANGEL ZERACHIEL

Archangel Zerachiel name means, "God's command". Archangel Zerachiel is known for his nurturing and loving presence, especially for children, animals, and the environment. One of the seven archangels named in the Book of Enoch, he is an Archangel primarily known for his healing abilities.

Archangel Zerachiel watches over children, especially those with parents who have addiction problems. He understands that for a child to grow up to be the best of themselves, it is essential to be nurtured in a loving, warm, and tolerant environment. Therefore, if your child, or a child you know, has a parent who struggles with any kind of addiction or aspect of their character which is contradictory to the warmth and nurturing a child needs, call upon Zerachiel to get involved and use his healing powers to help the child.

Zerachiel also helps both children and adults with nightmares. If you struggle with this, ask him to protect you. Where there are malevolent entities that terrorise you in your sleep, Zerachiel's protective light will help keep them away from you.

It is when we sleep that we are most susceptible to the spirit world because our conscious mind shuts down, and our subconscious mind takes over. It is the subconscious that provides a gateway, so remember, if you notice negative entities around you, call on Zerachiel to assist and help you.

He is also a protector and healer of animals and the environments. If an animal falls sick, call upon Zerachiel to help guide you and show you the way to help the animal. He is a fantastic angel to assist with those who are involved in the protection of the environment and want to see cleaner air, less pollution, and less plastic.

Zerachiel has a very nurturing presence, so for those who feel lost and alone, it is beneficial to call upon him. Loneliness can lead to sadness. He helps to soothe your inner child and guide you to a place where you no longer feel lonely or sad but cared for and loved.

Archangel Zerachiel helps with:

- Protecting children
- Healing animals and the earth.
- Healing and nurturing
- Healing addict
- Protection from night terrors
- Protection from nightmares
- Soothes loneliness

AFFIRMATION

Thank you, Archangel Zerachiel, for your
unconditional love and protection.
I am nurtured and loved.
My children are protected.
My animals are protected.
The earth is protected.
My animals are healed.
The earth is healed.
I am healed and protected.
I am loved and blessed.
I am surrendered by loving people.
I am filled with gratitude.
I am full of love.

Lord Jesus Christ

One of the greatest spiritual teachers and healers who ever walked the earth, Lord Jesus Christ, still lives with us today. His legacy lives on in the form of Christianity and millions of people all across the globe still look to him as a source of inspiration. The Son of God came to earth to show us the way - not to tell us what to think, who to worship or how to act, but rather to show us who we can be when we choose to become the very best of ourselves.

He encompasses love, kindness, compassion, truth, honour and justice, and was ultimately crucified for it. His suffering on the cross and the sacrifice made remains one of the greatest stories ever told. Each of us has the ability to be like Jesus. Inside of us exists a spirit and a soul which comes from the same place that Jesus, God and all the angels come from. No matter who we are or what background we hail from, we are at our best when we are doing good for others and when our intentions are motivated by selflessness, not selfishness. Jesus' teachings epitomised this. His teachings may have been twisted and tainted throughout the centuries, but the essence of him remains and touches each of us on a deep soul level, if we are willing to listen.

There are many ways we can call Jesus into our lives today. Naturally, we can visit a church and find him there; we can certainly celebrate his life, death, and resurrection. We do not need to do anything special to speak to Jesus or perform any elaborate ceremonies. Jesus is always with us and to speak to him, we only need to go inwards and call out for him. He will always listen and help you find the courage, strength, and wisdom within you.

When times are hard and you feel like giving up, call upon Lord Jesus Christ to help you get through the suffering. Remember when Jesus was mocked, reviled, and tortured just before his crucifixion and the subsequent agony he endured? Sometimes we, too, must go through great pain in order to come out on the other side. Great good can come from great suffering and Jesus will help to remind us of that when we face our own trials and tribulations. Calling Jesus into our lives can help us whenever we feel lost, confused, in pain or need strength and guidance to do what it is. You can call him anywhere at any time and he will stand by you, no matter what storms may come.

Lord Jesus Christ helps with:

- Compassion for others
- Strength in dark times
- Love for self and the world
- Peace on earth and goodwill to all
- Wisdom
- Finding your life purpose

- Seeing the positive in the negative
- Perseverance

AFFIRMATION

Thank You, Lord Jesus Christ, for Your
unconditional love and protection.
I am a compassionate and kind person.
Compassion is important.
I am strong through my trials.
I see the light at the end of the tunnel.
I love myself and others.
I show love to the world.
I am a light in this world.
I find peace on earth.
I find my inner wisdom.
I discover my life purpose.
I believe good will come from struggle.
I spread goodwill to all I meet.
This is a world of love and I am part of
that love.
I am compassionate and loving.
I am a powerful healer.
I bring peace and love wherever I go.
I am surrounded by love.

MOTHER MARY

A mother to all humans across the globe and most famously known as the mother of Jesus Christ, Mother Mary epitomises nurturing, kindness, compassion and sorrow in its purest essence.

Known also as the Virgin Mary, Our Lady of Lourdes, Our Lady of Heaven, Our Lady of Fatima, Our Lady of Sorrows, Our Lady of Africa and many other titles, Mother Mary is praised all across the world. She represents 'the mother 'in its entirety, encompassing the nature of a mother's love for her child (as she exhibited in the physical realm with her son, Jesus Christ) and the sorrow and joy that accompany motherhood, often in equal measure.

Mother Mary is there for us whenever we call out to her. Some people find it easier to contact her through praising her statue or visiting a place of worship where she is prominent, such as the church or Lourdes. But for other people, simply calling out her name is enough.

Mother Mary can help us whenever we are facing deep and challenging trials, particularly those related to motherhood, or situations where we must nurture and care for others.

In its purest essence, motherhood is something that exists within all of us, for it is the ability to love others unconditionally. Whether this exists between mother and child, father, and child, or human and the world, Mother Mary can help strengthen our hearts and resolve when things become too much for us to deal with. She exhibits grace and civility, promoting peace and union between lovers, friends, and communities. Mother Mary understands the trials of suffering well and she is always there to lay a hand on you when your own troubles burden you.

Mother Mary seeks unity between people of all races, colours and creeds, and is helpful for those seeking enlightenment within new cultures or countries, or where there is discord between nations or people. She helps bring wisdom and understanding, encouraging empathy as opposed to judgement.

The month of May is particularly potent in reaching out to Mother Mary. She represents new birth, childhood, innocence, and the birth of Spring. She can help those with childhood traumas heal and find their true path in the world, free from misery and suffering.

Mother Mary helps with:

- Unconditional love
- Love between parent and child
- Healing from childhood trauma
- Peace among different cultures
- Countries and creeds

- Wisdom and understanding
- Childbirth and nurturing
- Relief from suffering

AFFIRMATION

*Thank You, Mother Mary, for Your
unconditional love and protection.
I love my family unconditionally.
I love my child unconditionally.
Peace between all humans is what matters.
I believe in more empathy and less
judgement.
I am wise.
I am more understanding.
My struggles are a reminder that I am
strong and capable.
I nurture myself and others.
I heal from my childhood trauma.
My past experiences do not define me
today.
I am strong enough to move on from my
pain.
I believe in the gift of love.
I believe in the love of humanity.
I have a wonderful relationship with my
loved ones.
I love myself unconditionally.
I am loved.*

MARY MAGDALENE

Most famously known as the prostitute in the New Testament who followed Jesus Christ. Everything about Mary Magdalene has been distorted. She was one of Jesus closest disciples, and it believed that they were married. Mary Magdalene was one of Isis's students and was part of the White Brotherhood.

Mary Magdalene is associated with the Sacred Feminine and represents everything related to the feminine spirit: intuition, wisdom, strength from within and kindness.

Mary Magdalene lived in a time when a woman had a particular role, and any deviation from this role resulted in persecution and sometimes punishment by death. Throughout the ages, women have continued to be persecuted due to gender, and this still prevails in some countries today.

Therefore, Mary Magdalene is wonderful to call upon for all women who feel oppressed. Where one's individuality feels stifled or constricted, Mary can help them find their voice and call upon their own strength to find a way of expressing their unique individuality.

The struggle to release the Sacred Feminine in its real beauty can continue to be a struggle for many, and Mary Magdalene's wise and strong energy assists with this.

Mary Magdalene encourages all men and women, to embrace the Sacred Feminine within. There is pressure on men in male-dominated societies to conform with what is considered socially acceptable and with what a man should apparently be. This has led to a crackdown on the Feminine, and it is this imbalance that Mary helps to address.

To address this imbalance in the world, one must first be willing to address it within themselves. Change from the inside is what leads to change on the outside.

Mary Magdalene provides us with the strength and courage to do what is right, but not in a confrontational and aggressive way. Her energy is quiet confidence which does not use force to get what it wants. This is one of the truest forms of power.

She can be likened to two cards in the Tarot: Strength and the High Priestess. The Strength card shows a woman holding the mouth of a lion. The lion could easily eat her or bite her hand off, but her gentle calm and quiet strength keep the lion at bay. This is the strength of the Sacred Feminine.

The High Priestess represents the intuition and powers that come with it. The High Priestess is the card that shows the Feminine in its entirety. Intuition is often abandoned in favour of the rational mind in society, but its power is a very great one and one that everyone has access to if they choose to.

Because of her strong links to intuition, she is helpful to all practitioners of the occult. Today, in most countries, spiritual practitioners can practice and share their healing gifts with the world freely, without fear of retribution.

Mary Magdalene helps with:

- Connecting to the Sacred Feminine
- Bridging the gap between the Sacred Feminine and the Sacred Masculine
- Finding strength during troubled times
- Assists with finding your unique voice
- Nurturing your intuition
- Practitioners of the occult and witchcraft

AFFIRMATION

Thank you, Mary Magdalene, for your
unconditional love and protection.
I have strength and grace.
I am strong and powerful
I have my own unique voice
I connect to the Sacred Feminine
I merge the Sacred Feminine and Sacred
Masculine as one
I have powerful intuition
I nurture my magical abilities
I am love
I love and appreciate my healing gifts.

GUARDIAN ANGELS

Guardian angels are powerful beings in the spiritual realm who are assigned to us from the day we were born. Ultimately, they are messengers of God and protectors of humans, ready to assist us as we go through all the challenges we face on earth.

One of their most important duties is protecting people from danger. Guardian angels often work to guard us from danger in a number of ways. This may be in terms of an accident waiting to happen, or a situation we may be walking into that could have detrimental or fatal outcomes.

A guardian angel is not assigned to someone out of religious belief or lack of it; guardian angels protect and assist everyone, irrespective of belief. However, they also respect an individual's right of free will and to leave the individual if they desire it.

When we feel lost, alone, afraid, or have a challenging point in our life upon us, calling upon our guardian angels can help us stay safe and weather the storm, no matter how difficult it is or how much we want to give up hope.

Contacting our guardian angels can be done through meditation and ceremonial sessions with the use of crystals, incense, an alter and prayer, or it can be done at a place of worship or out among nature; it can be done through meditation before sleep so you can speak to them in your dreams, or it can be done wherever you are, without any special ritual, but merely your words that call out for help. Even if you cannot hear a reply from your guardian angel, know that they are there and working hard to protect you, guide you and keep you safe.

Guardian angels are also a direct link to God the Source of all, and they will pray for you when you are in need. They also help to strengthen your positive thoughts and positive energy, particularly when negative forces surround you.

Guardian angels are also responsible for recording your deeds on earth, both good and bad, so that when the time comes for you to leave and return to the Source, your life is kept record for you to look back on.

The battle of good and evil rages all over the earth, both inside us and outside of us. Guardian angels are there working for the light to keep us on the side of good and help us achieve our full potential.

Guardian Angels help with:

- Protecting us and keeping us safe
- Helping us find our path to God and the universe
- Helping us become the best of ourselves

- Prayer
- Recording our deeds

AFFIRMATION

Thank You, my Guardian Angels, for
Your unconditional love and protection.
I am protected and loved.
I call upon protection when I need it.
I face my challenges with ease.
I am connected to God and the universe.
I am the best of myself.
I know prayer helps me.
I do the best I can while alive.
I try to always help others.
I live with my heart and soul.
I know I am never alone.
I communicate with my guardian angels.
I involve my guardian angels with
everything I do.

SPIRIT GUIDES

Have you ever heard a voice whispering in your ear, but turned around and no one was there? Have you ever felt a presence with you, even though you were alone? Have you ever had a 'knowing 'or a 'feeling 'that something wasn't right or there was something specific you should do?

These could all be messages from your spirit guides. Our spirit guides are spirits who are assigned to us in order to assist and help us while we live on earth in our current physical incarnation. Some spirit guides are with us since birth, while others appear to us at various points in our lives to help us with whatever we are going through at the time. Spirit guides may have been humans who lived before, or they may even be other types of entities, such as elementals, fairies and paladins, beings who come from other realms and dimensions to assist here on earth. Some people have a few spirit guides; others have hundreds!

The purpose of the spirit guide is to help. When we ourselves come to earth, we become entrenched in the physical realm and many people often forget the spiritual side of themselves.

But it is always there, and it is what leads us to our true life-purpose. Spirit guides are there to help us remember our purpose and guide us towards it, especially if we have lost our way.

They help us realise what truly matters in life and they help us with everyday situations or problems, not just issues we have on a grand scale. If you have a problem with work, health, relationships, or anything in general, spirit guides are there to listen and guide you. It's like having your own personal agony aunt on hand!

Some people find it easier than others to listen to their spirit guides. Some may hear a voice out of the blue, see an image in their mind or simply just have a feeling. Others can contact their spirit guides through a meditation session or even in their dreams.

If you want to contact your guides, you simply just need to ask for their help and open your mind to whatever information comes through. Whatever problem you have and if you feel at a loss on what to do, your spirit guides can help show you the way.

Spirit Guides help with:

- Listening to your problems
- Guiding and assisting you
- Providing you with strength and wisdom to see your problems through
- Helping you find your true self and true path
- Steering you back on the right track

- Providing clarity and good judgment
- Understanding of patterns in the universe and how they work

AFFIRMATION

*Thank You, my Spirit Guides, for your
unconditional love and protection.
I am in contact with my spirit guides.
My spirit guides are here to help me.
I have assistance with my problems.
I am strong and wise.
I see things clearly.
I find my true self.
I find my life-purpose.
I judge my situations with clarity.
I understand how the universe works.
I understand why I am at this point in my
life.
I connect and hear my spirit guides easily.
I am guided and protected.*

SAGE PARAMAHANSA YOGANANDA

The Great Sage, Paramahansa Yogananda, was a mortal sage and one of the most revered spiritual teachers of the modern era. Introducing millions of Westerners and Indians to meditation and yoga, he is now prominently known as the Father of Yoga and has helped millions across the world discover their inner selves and learn harmony with it.

Uniting the Higher Self and the Lower Self is something that all humans must learn, though the paths they take to learn it may be different.

Yogananda was instrumental in helping people realise which path works best for them and bringing clarity and wisdom to them. Even after his death in 1952, his teachings remain abundant throughout the world, continuing to change the lives of many. Calling upon the spirit of Yogananda can help us communicate with God, the Universe and the Divine more clearly. It is easy for us to get so caught up in the physical and material world that we begin to lose sight of the spiritual one; for some people who are too caught up in the physical realm, the mere mention of the spiritual realm can cause them to wave their eyes and bat it away as if it were meaningless.

And yet, the spiritual realm is just as important as the physical one when it comes to helping us grow as individuals. We all have life lessons to learn here on Earth, hence why we came here in the first place.

Yogananda can help us find our way back to the spiritual path. Sometimes, our journey spiritually may be challenging and fraught with difficulty, but the path it leads us to is one of divine love and spiritual enlightenment.

He helps to heal us, spiritually, physically, and emotionally, but he also helps the world to heal too, promoting peace on every scale. Importantly, he encourages unity between religious beliefs. All religion comes from one source; it just manifests in different ways or it is infiltrated by a darkness that twists and manipulates its true teachings. Yogananda guides us toward seeing beyond what is obvious and looking deep beneath the surface.

And, of course, the great sage also promotes yoga practice, which everyone is encouraged to try as it helps bring about spiritual, mental, emotional, and physical balance and harmony to people's lives.

Yogananda helps with:

- Self-Realisation and Communication with God
- Divine love
- Spiritual, emotional, and physical healing
- Peace
- Unity between all religions
- Yoga practice and Kriya

AFFIRMATION

*Thank You, Yogananda, for Your
unconditional love and protection.
I communicate with God.
I hear God when he speaks to me.
I find divine love.
I heal on every level.
I heal my mind, body, and soul.
I am at peace with myself.
I am at peace with loved ones.
The world is in peace and in harmony.
All religion comes from the same source.
Religion is just another word for love.
Religions must unite to make the world a
better place.
I practice yoga.
Yoga helps bring peace and harmony to
my life.*

SAINT GERMAIN

Saint Germain is an ascended spiritual master, known widely for his wisdom and teachings of the Age of Aquarius that we have recently veered into. The Age of Aquarius brings significant change from the Age of Pisces, which was based around hierarchy and control from the external over the internal. Today, we can already see the effects of the Age of Aquarius taking place, which is all about equality and individuality of oneself, as opposed to identifying solely with an external force or label.

Saint Germain helps souls transcend to the New Age, and therefore, he is a good point of call for those who are breaking out of the restrictions previously or currently placed upon them as they seek their own individuality and life purpose. Such a transition can be painful and difficult as a number of sacrifices must be made. Saint Germain helps people ease in through this transition, bringing strength, wisdom and understanding as they go through this process.

As such, he is particularly helpful for those going into alchemy or who have an interest in it and need some guidance as to where to begin.

He is helpful when dealing with authority figures and for those embarking on leadership that includes influencing others, especially on a grand scale. He brings courage, direction, and purpose, helping to eliminate confusion and self-doubt, which are some of the biggest obstacles to finding one's true purpose. He provides people with the confidence to go forward with their endeavours and have no fear with what others may say or how they may judge.

Saint Germain can assist people with performing incredibly miraculous feats. If something seems impossible, He can bring magic and confidence to the individual to help make the impossible happen. He also provides extraordinary resilience and determination to the individual, so they do not give up, even when it seems all is lost.

His wealth of ability extends to protection from psychic negative forces, such as curses or people wishing ill on another. Calling on Saint Germain is also highly recommended when involved in clearing work, whether it is clearing yourself or your space. Invoking Saint Germain can help rid your space of negative energies both within yourself and in the environment surrounding you.

Saint Germain helps with:

- Alchemy
- Influencing people and authority figures
- Providing courage
- Direction and purpose
- Miraculous manifestations

- Perseverance
- Protection from psychic attack and space clearing

AFFIRMATION

Thank You, Saint Germain, for Your
unconditional love and protection.
I am a great alchemist.
I influence others for the higher good.
I am a good leader.
I deal with corrupt members of authority
with ease.
I am courageous.
I have direction.
I find my life purpose.
I manifest miracles in my life.
I manifest miracles into the world.
I am determined and driven.
I achieve anything I want to.
I am protected from psychic attacks.
I am protected from bad energies.
I create a healing space.
I heal myself from within.
I have a harmonious home.

GODDESS ABUNDANTIA

The Goddess Abundantia is the Goddess of Abundance. Those struggling with finances and money of all kinds would be wise to call on Abundantia for help and guidance.

Abundantia cannot wave a magic wand and make you a millionaire overnight, but she can help ease your burdens and help you on the path to prosperity so your fortunes change, bringing a little good luck your way. She can help things go a little more smoothly for you and give you the inner wisdom to realise whether you are making a good investment or not.

As the goddess of good fortune, she is particularly helpful to those who have been down on their luck lately. Anyone who has lost their job or found themselves out of pocket and struggling with basic necessities can call on Abundantia for help, to help bring them out of this dark situation and into the light.

However, green is not a quality that Abundantia advocates.

Money can corrupt just as easily as it can save; when an individual makes the transition from using money for the positive and into the negative, she can take away good fortune just as quickly as she bestowed it.

She is also very protective of our valuables and things that are dear to us. Some of these things can be expensive items, but others may be heirlooms or objects that have been handed down, generation to generation, and mean a great deal to us. Others may have cost nothing at all – perhaps a rock we picked up off a beach during a memorable, special day trip with a loved one, or a stick we picked up in the park while playing with a beloved dog. Anything that is of value to us, Abundantia will offer protection from loss, forgetfulness and thieves, helping us to safeguard the things that are dear to us and prevent the devastation or distress that comes with losing something we hold dear to our hearts.

All things money-wise are Abundantia's forte; money is something that every person worries about sometimes. Call upon Abundantia to take this worry and stress away from you, and to ease the pain that comes with it.

Goddess Abundantia helps with:

- Abundance
- Finances and investment
- Good fortunes
- Protecting valuables and things we hold dear to us

AFFIRMATION

Thank You, Goddess Abundantia, for
Your unconditional love and protection.
I create wealth in my life.
I have wealth in abundance.
I create abundance and joy in my life.
I use my wealth for the good of all.
I use my wealth to make my life better.
I make a wise investment.
I am clever with my finances.
I have savings for a rainy day.
I work towards my financial goals.
I attract good fortune.
Stress doesn't take over my money
situation.
I protect things dear to me.
My valuables are well-protected.
I am a magnet for miracles.
Money comes to me easily and frequently.

GODDESS APHRODITE

One of the most well-known among the Greek Goddesses, Aphrodite was famous for her breathtaking beauty and ability to strike romantic passion in the hearts of both men and Gods. According to Greek Mythology, her beauty was so powerful that many Gods believed it would ignite a war between the Gods themselves due to rivalry. Aphrodite herself had many lovers, both Gods and mortals.

The Goddess of Love and Beauty, Aphrodite, encompasses all things related to love, sex, beauty, attraction, and fertility. Relationships are one of the key functions of our lives, whether we are single or in a relationship ourselves, and therefore calling upon her assistance can greatly benefit us.

Anyone involved in a romantic relationship who is experiencing problems with commitment – either for themselves or their partner – would benefit from seeking Aphrodite's gentle energies which can help dissipate the fear of commitment or any anxiety surrounding it.

This fear is often deep-rooted and working with Aphrodite means working through these fears in order to find a path to happiness with the one you love.

She empowers all women to find the beauty within themselves and to make the most of their external beauty. She encourages taking care of oneself and appreciating the great beauty that each woman possesses. People who suffer from lack of confidence about their appearance can call upon Aphrodite to help them realise just how beautiful they truly are. She helps to bestow grace, inner wisdom and understanding of oneself and helps people to see themselves in a positive light, with a positive image.

Sex is a huge feature of Aphrodite as she represents the pleasures of both romantic and sexual union. Sex is meant to be enjoyed between two people who love each other deeply and if you experience sexual hang-ups, Aphrodite can help you overcome them so that you can have a healthy and happy sex life. Romantic passion and desire are normal parts of life and there is no shame in them as they can lead to great happiness and love, which is what Aphrodite endorses and what the world needs more of!

Goddess Aphrodite helps with:

- Commitment issues
- Engagement and marriage
- Femininity
- Beauty
- Grace
- Attraction
- Sexual issues
- Desire and romance

AFFIRMATION

*Thank You, Goddess Aphrodite, for Your
unconditional love and protection.
I am beautiful.
I am a person of beauty and grace.
I find my own beauty.
Beauty is subjective.
I have a loving, committed relationship.
I get over my commitment fears.
I help my beloved get over their
commitment fears.
I have a happy marriage.
I have a happy engagement.
I attract a partner I will love.
I attract a partner who will love me for
who I am.
I fix my issues with sex.
I help my loved one fix their issues with
sex.
I have a fulfilling sex life.
I find happiness through sex and
pleasure.
I find true romance.
I have desire and happiness in abundance.
I am beautiful and unique.*

GODDESS ARTEMIS

The Goddess Artemis is known as the "Goddess of the hunt"; she is one of the most revered of all the Goddesses in Ancient Greece.

The daughter of Zeus and twin sister of Apollo, Artemis is one of the most significant Goddesses for women and a protector of the young, vulnerable and those who cannot fend for themselves. She is the Goddess of virginity, childbirth, wild animals, and the great outdoors.

As a fierce and noble-hearted Goddess, Artemis is an inspiration to many for the strength and courage she encompasses, particularly in the face of adversity. Artemis represents life in its purest form and is quick to anger when anyone should harm of threaten that. This is why she is revered as the one who protects both wildlife and childbirth, a source of strength for those involved with the environment and raising children.

Those who seek help from Artemis can call upon her when they deal with issues within the environment or wild animals.

Many wild animals are under threat, such as the elephant, tiger, and pangolin; the environment is also under threat due to pollution and plastic. Anyone who raises concerns in these areas and wishes to help can call on Artemis's strength and protection to help them through the challenges they may face.

Similarly, Artemis helps all those involved with and assisting childbirth. She is deeply sympathetic to mothers, fathers, and midwives. Her caring energy helps bring calm and focus to situations which may be chaotic or fraught with nerves.

When you call upon Artemis, it can be in any form that feels comfortable to you. It can help to be outdoors while you do so, for Artemis loves the environment. An offering of spring water or wildflowers would be a lovely gesture of thanks. Sprinkling bird seed in your garden is a wonderful way of honouring Artemis, for all the little wild birds need feeding throughout the year!

Call upon Artemis's mighty and compassionate energy; she is ready to help you with anything you need.

Goddess Artemis helps with:

- Protecting the young and vulnerable
- Childbirth
- Wild animals and the environment
- Environmental activism
- Strength and courage in the face of danger

AFFIRMATION

*Thank You, Goddess Artemis, for Your
unconditional love and protection.
I protect the young and vulnerable.
I help the environment.
I help protect wildlife.
I help preserve nature and animals close
to extinction.
I am strong and bold enough to make a
change.
I face my challenges head-on.
I go forward with strength in my heart.
I am resourceful in chaotic moments.
I bring calm to stressful situations.
I deal with difficult situations with
strength and love.
I combat challenging tasks.
I help others be strong.
I help make the world better by protecting
it.*

GODDESS ATHENA

The Green Goddess Athena is the goddess of a number of things that are important and crucial to us in the world today. Originally known as the Goddess of War, Athena is particularly helpful for those who undergo conflict in their lives and seek wisdom and strength as attributes to help them get through.

We all have some form of conflict in our lives. Whether it is within our self, in our relationships, in society or on a global scale, conflict is a part of life that none of us can escape. What we can do, however, is choose how to deal with such conflict. We can sink into the deepest, darkest part of our own selves and become like the monsters we are trying to fight, or we can use the tools of love, compassion, and wisdom to shed light where there is darkness.

Athena is the patron of heroes of all kinds. Every one of us has the potential to be a great hero, but it is up to us whether we choose to go down this path or not.

Calling on Athena can bring us strength, wisdom, and perseverance. Sometimes we may become so disillusioned or distraught by our experiences that we want to give up.

Athena encourages us to keep going, no matter how hard things become.

Athena helps in resolving arguments so that a more mutually satisfying result can be achieved. She holds the scales of justice and helps us to see clearly what is right and what is wrong when the waters become muddied. Calling on Athena's great power can give us protection when we embark on dangerous missions, or situations that are challenging for us. She brings courage to us, helping us to become a beacon of light for others who may also be afraid.

Athena is also wonderful for helping writers, particularly those who are struggling with their creativity or suffering from writer's block. She helps remove blockages to our higher selves which access original ideas and helps us put pen to paper so we can articulate ourselves in the best possible way. She is a powerful Goddess who can make a true difference in our lives if we decide to call upon her.

Goddess Athena helps with:

- Resolving arguments
- Art, artists, crafts, and craftspeople
- Attaining justice
- Physical and psychological
- Protection
- Avoiding and resolving war
- Writers and writing

AFFIRMATION

*Thank You, Goddess Athena, for Your
unconditional love and protection.
I am brave and strong.
I handle all the challenges I face.
I find a way through the conflict.
I resolve arguments peacefully.
I direct my energies where they need to
go.
I walk away from conflict that is
unnecessary.
I attune into my art.
I write beautifully.
I am a writer with much creativity.
I beat my writer's block.
Peace is my goal.
I am protected from the dark forces.
I protect others who are suffering.*

GODDESS BRIGIT

The Celtic Goddess Brigit is also known as the Goddess of the Flame. Her name means "exalted one" or "she who is on high". She is one of the goddesses associated with warriors and her warrior attributes revolve mostly around protection and courage.

She is associated with seers and prophets, healers, and herbalists, helping them to see their path clearly so they may become the truest form of themselves for the greater benefit of mankind. Brigit helps all people find their life purpose. Very often, we can become stuck, not knowing why we are here or what our own unique gifts should be used for. Brigit brings us clarity, wisdom, and insight. The process may be slow and, at times, challenging, but the Goddess of the Flame helps ease us through the transition, minimising negative associations as much as possible.

Brigit represents the dual nature of humanity as she is described as being 'beautiful and light ' on one side and 'dismal and ugly ' on the other. She teaches us that we all have a dark side and yet running from it or pretending it is not there is a surefire way for it to seize control of us.

Brigit helps us unite both our light and dark sides so that we may become whole, to become the masters of ourselves so we may raise the vibration of the planet and do our best for this world.

Brigit is said to be the ultimate caretaker of birth and fertility, providing extra protection to mothers and babies, particularly during difficult births. She is also a significant factor in relationships, helping to provide warmth and companionship, particularly for those who are unhappy in their relationships or who feel alone. Because she is strongly associated with the environment, she is also a distinct ally of Mother Nature, helping to protect the animals, trees, oceans, and lands that our world is made up of. She encourages compassion for all living creatures and towards each other. Brigit helps with self-esteem, aiding people in self-love and an acceptance of who we are.

Calling on Brigit's power can help us become more fulfilled individuals who find our life's purpose, providing us with the strength, compassion, and wisdom to fulfil our highest destinies.

Goddess Brigit helps with:

- Courage
- Finding our Life Purpose and finding direction
- Protection
- Warmth in relationships
- Acceptance of our bodies
- Helping the environment

AFFIRMATION

*Thank You, Goddess Brigit, for Your
unconditional love and protection.
I am strong and powerful.
I am a courageous person.
I am gifted and I use my gifts wisely.
I am the best of myself.
I find my life purpose.
I fulfil my destiny.
I find who I truly am.
I acknowledge both the light and the
shadow.
I have wonderful relationships with
others.
I accept who I am.
I love myself.
I am happy with who I am.
I love this world and I protect it.
I protect animals and the environment.*

GODDESS CORDELIA

The beautiful Goddess Cordelia is the Goddess of fairies, Spring and Summer. Cordelia is also the daughter of Lir, the Sea God, and is therefore intrinsically connected to the seas, oceans, and many bodies of water.

Cordelia's connection with nature helps us find our own deep link to the sea, sky, land and air. Particularly, many who dwell within cities find themselves disconnected with nature and may feel like they are suffocating from the smog of city life and metropolitan stress. It can be very soothing and healing to connect to Cordelia who helps us reconnect with the divine inside ourselves.

Stress does not have to be a part of our lives. No matter how stressful things become, we have a choice: we can fall into the stress and make it a part of us, or we can keep stress separate from ourselves. This is the gift we possess as human beings – the choice whether to allow negative energy to become part of us or not.

As Cordelia is a Goddess of the outdoors, we connect best with her when we ourselves are out among nature.

The forests, woods, trees, flowers, plants – Cordelia's spirit exists within all of them and is there to help us, if we should ask for her help.

She loves to see us celebrating and being happy as human beings. Sadness, stress, and negative emotions are just as devastating for her as they are for us; she wants us to be happy, hence why she wishes to spread love and goodwill to all. If you are celebrating a wedding, birthday, national holiday, or any other type of event to celebrate, call on Cordelia for extra love, joy, and happiness to brighten your day all the more.

Flowers and gardens love Cordelia, so if you are trying your hand at gardening or caring for your own personal plants, bless them with Cordelia's love for extra growth and guidance. A plant that is dying or has sadly died should be placed back into the earth with Cordelia's love and blessings attached.

Plants, just like humans and animals, share this world with us, and as the most intelligent species, we have a duty to protect every sentient being of this planet. She gives us the strength, courage, and compassion to do so.

Goddess Cordelia helps with:

- Celebration
- Courage
- Flowers and gardening
- Life changes and stress management

AFFIRMATION

*Thank You, Goddess Cordelia, for Your
unconditional love and protection.
I connect easily with the flower fairies.
I am having a wonderful day.
I celebrate new life on earth.
I celebrate this union with those I love.
I celebrate this day with love and joy in
my heart.
I focus my dominant thoughts on the
things I want.
I easily release stress from my life.
I remain calm and cool.
I protect nature.
I protect the plants and animals.
I enjoy my life and experiences.
I am loving and peaceful.
I make this world beautiful with my
respect for nature.
I face new challenges with strength and
courage.*

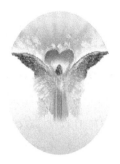

GODDESS DAMARA

The Goddess Damara, also known as the Queen of the Fairies and whose name means "gentle", holds special resonance with the month of May. Damara is associated with health, fertility, abundance, and kindness. She represents all things new, fresh, and innocent. May is the time when the animals come out of hibernation, when new life is at its most prominent and when the earth is reborn as the flowers, trees and plants begin to blossom and bloom. She is particularly special for the fields, herds, and flocks, bringing good luck and fortune to those who invoke her powers to help with their own abundant fields and land.

A Celtic Goddess of Great Britain, Damara rules creativity, innocence, and imagination. Hence, she is intimately connected, not only to children, but to the inner child within all of us. She is a protector of children and a defender of our inner child, helping to keep it alive. Many of us may find ourselves running the risk of losing our inner child as we grow older, primarily when the stress and heaviness of life brings us down. We forget who we truly are and therefore can forget the inner child inside of us.

Calling upon Damara helps us remember who we are and bring the innocence out of us, which automatically tackles the darker side of our ego that all of us struggle with. Only through the eyes of a child can we regain a sense of purpose and wonderment, which is crucial to our overall existence as human beings.

Damara also brings peace to feuding families or a home seeped in negative energy due to conflict or bad feeling. She can help heal wounds between families, promoting forgiveness, compassion, understanding and love, breaking down the ego and reminding everyone of what truly matters. Scores can be settled, and love can be renewed when Damara's presence is called upon in the family home.

Damara also assists with manifestation and the belief that one's thoughts can lead to something real and tangible in the real world. Manifestation is intrinsically connected to our inner child. She encourages us to connect with this deep part of ourselves — the innocent imaginative side of us that knows no boundaries in the imagination, so that we may create our own realities as we wish and live the life we want.

Goddess Damara helps with:

- Abundance
- Children, guiding and healing
- Peaceful home
- Manifestation

AFFIRMATION

Thank You, Goddess Damara, for Your
unconditional love and protection.
I have the happy life that I want.
I am connected to my inner child.
I protect the children of this world.
I protect the child inside of me.
I am a creative being.
My imagination knows no limits.
I make peace with my family.
I have abundance in crops and fields.
I settle old scores and move on.
I forgive those who wronged me.
I forgive myself.
I am at peace with myself.
I keep my inner child alive.
I have the life I dream of.

GODDESS DANA

The Goddess Dana means, "knowledge" and her powers and attributes are centered around this very thing. Dana is an extremely powerful Celtic goddess that revolves around creation and origin.

Goddess Dana seeks to show mankind that every single one of us is a 'God' and 'Goddess' in our own way. The danger begins when mankind combines arrogance and pride with this knowledge; the knowledge that one is a 'God' or a 'Goddess' has nothing to do with power over others, but instead the understanding that we are all wise beings filled with love and compassion, and this is what makes one a true deity – not power over any other person. Instead, humility is the most important aspect that comes with this knowledge, and Goddess Dana helps to inform us of the great power that lies within us. Dana is the ultimate goddess of magic. She helps us connect with our own deep link to magic itself, which has been long lost in the modern world. This is why she is particularly helpful for spell-weavers, alchemists, and healers of all sorts.

She helps those who are seeking to perform manifestation, the ability to transform thoughts into reality.

Dana is profoundly connected with nature and therefore helps the animals and our work with animals. She helps us to love and respect the creatures of this earth. She is also a goddess who cares greatly about children and mothering and helps to assist mothers who are about to give birth or who are trying for a child.

Because Goddess Dana is also the goddess of magic, she is connected to other Beings who exist in this world, but who not everyone can see – in particular, the elementals. Elementals can be Beings such as leprechauns or fairies who are all around us, assisting and guiding us in their own special way. Invoking Goddess Dana's gifts can help us connect with the elementals and ask them to show us the way when we may be lost or confused. Goddess Dana assists us with the greatest love of all – the love we have for our own self. Anyone who suffers from lack of confidence or low self-esteem would benefit from calling upon Dana. She teaches self-love and self-care, reminding us that we are all kings and queens in our own right and that we deserve our own love and respect.

Goddess Dana helps with:

- Abundance
- Alchemy
- Divine magic
- Animals
- Children and motherhood
- Meeting and working with the elementals
- Self-worth and self-love

AFFIRMATION

Thank You, Goddess Dana, for Your
unconditional love and protection.
I work with divine magic.
I manifest my heart's desire.
I create abundance in my life.
I am a great Being of love and light.
I am a God/Goddess in my own right.
I bear children.
I take care of children.
I work with the elementals.
I am a worthy person.
I love myself.
I am beautiful and wonderful.
I deserve to be loved.
I deserve to be happy.
I think positive things about myself.

GODDESS GUINEVERE

Known primarily in Arthurian Legend as the Queen of Camelot and wife of King Arthur, Guinevere is also a goddess, moreover a Goddess of the Land. Legend says that Guinevere was greatly sought for by the greatest knights in the kingdom, but it was Arthur who won her heart. As the Queen of the Round Table, she serves as a great inspiration to Mankind, helping individuals believe in their own power and urging them to achieve anything they dare to dream.

Goddess Guinevere, while a mortal on earth and married to King Arthur and engaging in a love affair with Sir Lancelot, the greatest knight of all, naturally has an inclination toward romance and love. Hence, she is a great help to those who seek love and romance, and who suffer from loneliness and solitude that they wish they could change. Guinevere helps people find their beloved and soulmate, guiding them gently to the one who can help them feel complete.

She helps to keep the belief of romance alive. As we grow older, we may encounter broken relationships and broken hearts. This can lead us to becoming cynical and cold.

We may doubt love itself, closing our hearts so that even when we find someone who could truly make us happy, we do not allow ourselves to become one with this. Unwittingly, we may destroy our own dream of love and our desire for happiness by becoming the very thing that stands in the way of finding true love. Goddess Guinevere helps us break the boundaries of doubt in love; she helps to melt a heart of ice and helps people see beyond their fears, insecurities, jealousy, resentment, bitterness, or anger. Invoking her spirit can help us to return to the innocence we once had when we dreamed of a fairytale love; calling upon her assistance can help us attract this type of love into our life and help us be the best of ourselves so we may aid and cherish it in all its preciousness.

Goddess Guinevere also helps with women's issues, helping women to feel strong and confident no matter what situation they find themselves in, whether it be relationships, motherhood, work, or anything else that women need strength and courage to endure. Calling upon her spirit helps us channel her energy and lead us towards a path of well-being, happiness, and enlightenment.

Goddess Guinevere helps with:

- Finding and enhancing romantic love
- Breaking through barriers that prevent true love
- Understanding our own capacity to love another
- Assisting with women's issues
- Inspiration

- Belief in ourselves
- Tenacity to achieve our hopes and dreams

AFFIRMATION

*Thank You, Goddess Guinevere, for Your
unconditional love and protection.
I am with the love of my dream.
I conquer my bitterness and past hurts.
I find my soulmate.
I love being in love.
I overcome my broken heart.
I love another with my heart and soul.
I love unconditionally.
I believe in myself.
I achieve anything I want to achieve.
I am capable of anything I dream of.
I overcome any hurdles in my way.
I am love and I am lovable.*

GODDESS HATHOR

The Goddess Hathor is a famous goddess of Ancient Egypt. Known as the Lady of the Stars, worship of Goddess Hathor was both widespread and devoted. Today, many seek Hathor for help in a variety of areas of their life.

Hathor is one who appreciates beauty and bestows beauty to those who call upon her assistance. She promotes attractiveness and cosmetics to enhance beauty that is already there. Though some may mistake this for vanity or shallowness, this is not the case at all. Rather, She promotes the type of beauty where one is comfortable in their own skin and exudes a shining light of self-confidence and approval of one's own self – this is the true beauty that exists and one that She can help others to see, particularly those who struggle with low self-confidence or low self-esteem.

She helps us to understand that the creative arts and the soul are intertwined as one. Many of her priests were dancers and musicians. She helps creative spirits use their creativity to help them find the path to the Source, to the Love and Light that exists in this world and that there is no shame in any of their gifts.

Celebrations abound, anyone who is looking forward to a party and night of dancing can call upon Hathor who loves such events! She adores it when people are having a good time together and indulging in the pleasures of life, which bring happiness and sensuality in harmonious synchronicity.

Hathor teaches us that life is to be lived and pleasure is a part of life.

She also assists women who are trying to get pregnant, just as she assists those who are already pregnant or parenting. A welcome support for doubtful or tired parents, she helps with encouragement and providing strength when weariness takes hold.

For those who seek their soulmate, she is wonderful to call upon. Life can be lonely and many of us would love to find that special someone who helps us feel complete. Hathor can guide us and gently push us in the right direction, helping us find that special someone – and more often than not, it may not be the person we would expect!

Goddess Hathor helps with:

- Beauty and attractiveness
- Artistic pursuits
- Celebrations, parties, and dancing
- Children, pregnancy, and conceiving
- Parenting
- Making decisions
- Finding true love and soulmates

AFFIRMATION

Thank You, Goddess Hathor, for Your
unconditional love, and protection.
I am beautiful.
I am beautiful on the inside and outside.
I am a star.
I have creative ambition.
I am a creative person.
I mix the spiritual and creativity.
I have a great time celebrating.
Life is for living.
Life is for celebrating.
Pleasure is my birthright.
I am a wonderful parent.
I am a loving and nurturing parent.
I make the right choice.
I find my one true love.
I am happy with my soulmate.

GODDESS ISHTAR

A Sumerian Goddess of war and fertility, the Goddess Ishtar was an enormous inspiration during the time of Ancient Babylon. It is said that Ishtar possessed an extreme side of both light and dark. She could promote great love, peace and fertility or she could be jealous, promoting war, infertility, and vengeance on those who wronged her or her people. Today, Ishtar is one of the best goddesses to help with a variety of issues, particularly ones which tend to linger beneath the surface and are not so obvious to the all-seeing eye.

Ishtar is particularly good for those seeking child conception. She is one of the primary goddesses of fertility and blesses those who call upon her for assistance in this area. She also assists in the process of parenthood, which can be both challenging and deeply rewarding in equal measure, and helps parents, especially new ones, find a semblance of harmony and peace in their child-rearing endeavors.

As one of the main goddesses of Ancient Babylon, she is also one of the most compassionate. Her compassion was just as legendary as her fury.

Ishtar promotes healing of all kinds and can help people heal — mentally, physically, and emotionally. Sometimes, a deep wound can last for years, affecting the way we go about our lives and how we treat both ourselves and others; Ishtar helps the individual heal these wounds so we can be the happiest and most wholesome versions of ourselves. She promotes gentleness with oneself, encouraging us to love ourselves and not be too hard on ourselves or one another. In doing so, she helps us become the best of ourselves when it comes to loving relationships with others, helping to dissolve ego that can get in the way of a true connection.

Known as the goddess of war, Ishtar excels in this area. If we find ourselves going to war, whether with ourselves or others, we can call upon Ishtar to provide us with strength and courage. If we would prefer to avoid war and rather seek diplomatic means of resolution, she can also help in preventing conflict. Simultaneously, she harnesses strong powers against harmful lower entities that can attach themselves to us and feed on our worst fears and own negative feelings; She helps to remove these entities and stop them from latching onto us once they are in our vicinity.

Ishtar is also profoundly connected to the weather; if you are hoping for an event with bright sunny skies, call on Ishtar to help you manifest the perfect day!

Goddess Ishtar helps with:

• Fertility and parenting

- Compassion
- Healing
- Gentleness
- Marriage and loving relationships
- Protection against harmful energies
- Sexuality
- War and the prevention of war
- The weather

AFFIRMATION

*Thank You, Goddess Ishtar, for Your
unconditional love and protection.
I am a wonderful parent.
I take good care of my child.
I love my child unconditionally.
I am a compassionate being.
I deserve to be loved.
I am a wholesome, beautiful person.
I find love with another.
I am happy in my marriage.
I create compromise in my
marriage/relationship.
I am protected against lower energies.
I am victorious.
I find a way other than direct conflict.
I enjoy my life and every day is a
beautiful day.
I am good at diplomacy.
I am loved and protected.*

GODDESS ISIS

The Goddess, Isis, was one of the most powerful deities of Ancient Egypt. As the mother of Horus, she wields a large amount of powerful healing magic that is particularly linked to the divine feminine. Hence, she remains to this day an important goddess for women and for all womanly matters.

A highly protective goddess, Isis is intrinsically linked with divine magic. The source of all life is the divine magic, and it exists within each and every one of us. Manifesting our thoughts into reality is part of this divine magic; loving ourselves and one another is divine magic; creating new life, both physically and metaphorically, is divine magic.

Isis helps us to connect to this magic, which can so often be lost as we become entrenched within our daily lives. We become so focussed on the external that we forget about the internal. We forget about our own divine magic and instead focus on "outer magic" as it is perceived in society. We exist to do the bidding of others, rather than the bidding of ourselves.

It is only when we unlock this potential within ourselves that we can become who we were meant to be.

Isis is one of the best deities to help us with this. Her powerful magic is both soothing and compassionate. Working with her is to have one of the greatest mentors and teachers in the realm of magic, bringing us confidence and strength in our understanding of our abilities.

Isis is, as mentioned above, a goddess of the feminine. She helps women (and men) embrace their feminine side. She is particularly important at this time. In the past, it was seen as shameful if men were to show their emotions, such as crying in public; today, feminine energy is slowly making its way as an equal to masculine energy and calling upon Isis can help each individual harness their own unique feminine energy within them. She brings power and beauty to those who call upon her for help, helping people to find the beauty of life, while harnessing and understanding despair and why it exists. Isis helps us with our own inner selves and enables us to feel a sense of self-esteem. Those suffering with low self-confidence and lack of esteem can call upon Isis to help them realise their own self-worth. We are all special, unique beings of the Divine; what we must do is recognise this. Calling upon Isis can help us believe it.

Goddess Isis helps with:

- Divine magic
- Feminine strength and power
- Beauty, personal joy, and self-esteem
- Mother and child relationship
- Healing

AFFIRMATION

*Thank You, Goddess Isis, for Your
unconditional love and protection.
I harness my own divine magic.
I understand myself and my abilities.
I embrace my feminine and masculine.
I embrace my feminine energy to do good
in the world.
I manifest my thoughts into reality.
I am a beautiful person.
I am a powerful person.
I am worthy of love and acceptable.
I build my confidence and self-esteem.
I find happiness within myself.
I am strong and powerful.
I am confident and beautiful.
I am loving and joyful.
I am a powerful healer.
I love my uniqueness.
I love and accept myself just as I am.*

GODDESS ISOLT

For lovers, relationships, and all things romantic and sexual, Goddess Isolt is one of the best deities to call upon. Legend says that Isolt existed during the time of King Arthur and she began a passionate love affair with Tristan, the prince of Cornwall. Since then, Isolt has earned her place as a goddess, helping all of us here on earth finding our way when it comes to romantic love.

An energetic force, she is a beam of light with the ability to assist in all matters of the heart. It is part of our life journey as humans to experience relationships with others and one of the most potent of these relationships is the romantic kind. Feelings such as love, intensity, jealousy, possessiveness and many more, both on the negative and positive end of the spectrum, can empower or destroy us in a love relationship. Isolt helps us to understand these emotions, gently guiding us as we sift our way through the heart and its many twisting realms.

She helps those who are seeking love. If you feel that loneliness dominates your life, Isolt can help you find a companion, one who can satisfy both your carnal and romantic needs.

She is spectacular in helping to ignite passion, particularly in partnerships where passion appears to have died or turned into a very weak flame. If you are looking for some spice and action in your marriage or relationship, invoke Isolt and watch the flames sparkle once more!

Isolt does not just aid in relationships, but also in the demise of them. The breakup of a relationship or partnership can be one of the most devastating things we as humans experience. A broken heart can last for many years; in some extreme cases, it never mends. She can help mend a broken heart and heal those who have suffered from separation or divorce, enabling them to find love again.

She is one of the greatest goddesses for promoting enduring love that lasts, rather than whimsical fancy. If love is a missing part of your life or if you feel something isn't quite right in your love life, call upon Isolt to help show you the way and lead you to a path of true fulfilment and happiness.

Goddess Isolt helps with:

- Healing from separations, breakups, and divorce
- Reigniting passion in relationships
- Attraction and romantic love

AFFIRMATION

Thank You, Goddess Isolt, for Your
unconditional love and protection.
I find true love.
I find my other half.
I am happy in love.
I open my heart to others.
I heal from my breakup.
I heal the pain in my heart.
I free my heart from the ice lodged there.
I bring passion to my relationship.
I reignite the flames in my relationship.
I continue igniting passion in my
relationship.
I attract a wonderful partner.
I give new love a chance.
I am in love.
I let love back into my life.
It is easy for me to find love.

GODDESS KALI

The Goddess, Kali, is a Hindu Goddess who has been somewhat misunderstood throughout history. There has been an association with fear when it comes to Kali due to her intrinsic links to violence, sexuality, and death. In fact, being the Goddess of Death is what has given her this feared reputation.

But there is nothing to fear; yes, Kali is intertwined with death, but not the death that we feel is associated with all that is bad and frightening. Instead, she represents the death of the ego, the side of ourselves that we often wrestle with and the side which often presents obstacles in our path in our quest to become the best and brightest versions of ourselves.

The battle between the soul and the ego is one we all go through to some degree. In astrology, the sign of Scorpio represents the war between the higher and lower selves and the ultimate victory of the soul over the ego, hence why Scorpio is often shown as a phoenix rising from the ashes. Because of this, Kali is especially helpful for those born under the Rising Sun or Moon signs of Scorpio.

Kali brings determination, drive and focus to those who call upon her assistance. Strongly associated with fear, Kali brings courage where there is cowardice, and strength where there is weakness. She finely tunes the dark sides of our self, drawing them into the open so they may unite with the light and ultimately be conquered by it. This is why those who do battle with themselves and others benefit greatly from Kali's strength and determined energies. She is able to motivate those who lack motivation. She reminds us to never give up, even when it seems all hope is lost.

She lends protection to those who need it. A goddess that fully understands the dark and light, she assists those going into places angels dare not tread, helping the individual to realise that in order to overcome one's own darkness, they must first walk the path of darkness and see it reflected outside of them. Only then can one understand the darkness within them, vanquish it and, in turn, become a beacon of light for others. Kali is the Goddess of the ending of cycles and transformation energy that lets go of the old and brings in the new. When you face struggles, battles, and demons in your life, call upon the power of Kali to aid you in your war and help you become victorious.

Goddess Kali helps with:

- Courage, direction, and focus
- Determination
- Understanding the battle between soul and ego
- Assisting in the war between the higher and lower self

- Motivation
- Tenacity
- Protection

AFFIRMATION

Thank You, Goddess Kali, for Your
unconditional love and protection.
I conquer my lower self.
I transform myself.
I rise above the ashes.
I conquer my ego.
I am the best of myself.
I help others become the best of
themselves.
I am brave.
I am determined.
I am strong.
I am powerful.
I am protected.
I continue learning and evolving.
I strive on till the end.
I focus on what services me.
I remove negative energy from my life.
I am a beacon of light.

GODDESS KUAN YIN

The Goddess, Kuan Yin, is most famously known as the Goddess of Compassion and Mercy. A Goddess of Buddhism, she encompasses a Divine light that is gentle, healing, and powerful all rolled into one.

Compassionate individuals or those seeking to become more compassionate would benefit greatly from invoking Kuan Yin into their life. Her kindness and clemency radiate powerful energy. It is the same energy that compels a stranger to help someone on the street who is suffering, the same energy that gives people the ability to feel the pain of others as if it were their own, and to take action to put a stop to that pain. The very same energy that gives us the power of self-sacrifice, the most noble of all human qualities.

Compassion is not just the feeling of distress that overcomes us when we see the suffering of another; it is also the desire to act upon that feeling. Kuan Yin encourages us to do whatever is within our power to help end the suffering of others. Benevolence and kindness are at the heart of her energies. The more we are filled with compassion and kindness, the more whole we become as individuals.

Kuan Yin is also the Goddess of Mercy. Those who are struggling with forgiveness or who feel bitterness seep into their heart due to wrongdoing done to them or others would do well to call on her energies. She can melt a heart of ice and help us understand that, when all is said and done, when the ice has melted and the clouds have parted, there is only love — love for ourselves and for one another. Love does not judge or have any desire to hurt others, no matter what wrong has been done to us. This is the epitome of Mercy.

Those with musical abilities would also benefit from invoking the power of Kuan Yin. Music is a way for people to express the very deepest part of their souls, things that cannot be expressed in words. Kuan Yin helps the musically gifted enhance their abilities and produce art that the world can share and enjoy, basking in the beauty of 'soul-speak 'which is essentially what music is.

Possessing great abilities of protection when we embark upon the road of compassion, Kuan Yin protects those who walk the path of clemency and kindness. If we feel fear or anxiety in our journey, calling upon her assistance can help give us strength and courage.

Goddess Kuan Yin helps with:

- Compassion
- Clairvoyance
- Receiving and giving kindness
- Mercy
- Musical abilities

- Protection
- Spiritual enlightenment

AFFIRMATION

*Thank you, Goddess Kuan Yin, for your
unconditional love and protection.
I am a compassionate person.
I am kind.
I am gifted.
I help others with my gifts.
I have a big heart and help others.
I have musical talent.
I use my talent to create beautiful music.
I am protected from dark forces.
Love triumphs all else.
I am a merciful person.
I believe in mercy.
I am profoundly clairvoyant.
I am enlightened.*

GODDESS LAKSHMI

For those seeking improvement in their fortunes or who feel down on their luck in regard to the household or material aspect of life, Goddess Lakshmi can help bring them abundance, wealth, and prosperity.

The Hindu Goddess, Lakshmi, has been revered for centuries due to her powers of manifestation. Manifestation is the ability to transform mental thought into the physical realm. One example of this is the God of the Old Testament who said,' Let there be light' and light appeared.

Manifestation is something we are all capable of to some degree. As long as we are manifesting with positive intent and no negative ill-will towards others or ourselves, then we can enjoy manifestation in abundance. Lakshmi helps people bring their dreams into reality using the power of their thoughts. Of course, as mentioned, the intent must be pure. A person who wishes for riches and finery, all with the intention to appear 'better 'than others or to spend it on things which could cause harm, not only to others, but also to their own soul, will not be able to reap the benefits of manifestation in the way it is intended to be.

But the desire for wealth in order to make oneself a better person or the world a better place shall be granted to the soul that is pure and true.

Invoking Lakshmi can bring good luck and abundance to those who call upon her. Struggle does not have to be necessary when it comes to the material world.

The amount of stress and sickness that occurs as a result of financial or house problems is striking in today's world. Call upon Lakshmi to help alleviate this distress and make your life happier and more abundant. The removal of stress can make for a much more peaceful and happier life, which is how life is meant to be lived. It is a cycle that many people tend to feel trapped in; calling upon Lakshmi can help break this cycle.

She also helps with space in the home. Clutter and mess can be another great contributor to stress. Invoking Lakshmi can help people create space that can bring them peace of mind and greater harmony in the household.

Goddess Lakshmi helps with:

- Beauty
- Aesthetics
- Abundance
- Happiness
- Space clearing for the home
- Manifestation

Affirmation

Thank you, Goddess Lakshmi, for Your
unconditional love and protection.
I am beautiful.
I have a beautiful home.
I am free of monetary worries.
I am wealthy and happy.
I have abundance.
I use my wealth to help others.
I am happy in my life.
I release stress from my life.
I manifest anything I choose.
I make my dreams come to life.
I have a happy home.
I am at peace in my home.
I am prosperous.

GODDESS MAAT

If it is truth and justice you seek, then look no further than the Goddess Maat. A Goddess of Ancient Egypt, Maat was known widely for her representation of justice, truth, and morality. She was the daughter of the great Egyptian God, Ra, and the wife of Thoth, the Moon God. She was the ultimate authority in justice of all kinds, whether on Earth or in the afterlife. Maat would decide where a soul would go in the afterlife, weighing up their actions while they lived and deciding on the next suitable path with them, according to her own personal values of truth, justice, and balance.

Like the scales of Libra in Western Astrology, Maat represents the understanding that everything in life has cause and effect, and that balance is the ultimate goal to equilibrium. Maat is particularly good for Librans who sometimes struggle with weighing up pros and cons in life and finding harmony and balance. She can help them as they travel through their own soul's journey, helping them to understand that harmony and balance is achievable—once one fully comprehends all aspects of both sides.

Maat is helpful to anyone who is having trouble separating the truth from the lie. In a time where the truth is increasingly becoming difficult to see, she is important now more than ever. She helps bring clarification and wisdom to those who are struggling to see past the surface. Often, people will accept what is on the surface as the ultimate truth, but more often than not, this is not the case. Calling upon Maat can help clear the debris of falsehood away until only the truth remains.

Likewise, she is extremely helpful in protecting against manipulation and deceit. Wars are often fought with words these days and soldiers are recruited based on what they believe, this belief stemming from what they are told. When falsehood dominates, this only perpetuates a state of evil which can be difficult to unravel once it takes hold. Maat is able to protect individuals from being manipulated so they do not fall into this trap. She can help people connect with their own Divine Spirit which will keep them close to the truth at all times.

Her determination to uphold truth and justice in this world is paramount; call upon Maat when you feel uncertain, lost, and confused, and she will help show you the way. Maat is also extremely helpful for those struggling with addictions and cravings of all kinds, helping them to overcome these debilitating habits and seeking a path of wholeness and wellness.

Goddess Maat helps with:

- Clarification of confusing situations

177

- Integrity
- Finding the truth and separating truth from lies
- Divine magic
- Commitment and orderliness
- Overcoming addictions
- Protection against manipulation and deceit
- Purifying the body

AFFIRMATION

Thank You, Goddess Maat, for your
unconditional love and protection.
I am a truth seeker.
I find the truth among the lies.
I separate the truth from the false.
I overcome my addictions.
I combat my cravings.
I am a person of integrity.
I am a person of morals.
I am a person of honour.
I create order out of chaos.
I am protected from manipulation.
I am a pure being.
I connect to my own Divine Magic.
I am committed to the truth.
I am committed to justice.
I am honest and trustworthy.

GODDESS MAEVE

The epitome of warrior queens everywhere, the Goddess Maeve is an Irish Goddess famed for her strength, courage, beauty, and sexual prowess. A sovereign goddess, she lived a colourful life, exhibiting her skills in war, her ability to use any resource as a weapon - even her sex - and also her jealousy and ruthlessness.

Maeve is a particularly potent goddess for women everywhere, especially those who are struggling to find their inner strength or inner goddess. Calling upon her gifts means to call upon her own supreme powers of strength and fortitude. She provides beauty, attractiveness and confidence to women who struggle with loving themselves or find themselves in situations where these qualities may be particularly necessary.

Because Maeve is strongly connected to nature, she has an intricate relationship with the Elementals, who are all around us but whom few can see. However, more often than not, they are here to guide and help us and Maeve can provide communication between us and them.

If you feel an Elemental nearby, do not hesitate to call on Maeve to help you hear what they are trying to say!

Still in line with her strong relationship with nature, she also assists those who are interested in, or practicing, herbology, helping them to differentiate between various herbs and giving them confidence in their concoctions. Likewise, she assists alchemists and aromatherapists – any role that includes using natural resources to help heal and soothe. This also extends to the role of healing itself. Maeve can help practitioners and students of the healing arts to have confidence in their abilities and recognise the pinpoint areas when it comes to diagnosis.

The Goddess of Horses, Maeve has a special relationship with them and assists in protecting and healing them. As a warrior queen, horses were a crucial part of her existence, assisting her in her wars and battles; as a goddess, her love of them is no different. If you need help with a horse or wish to understand them better, she can assist you.

Those struggling with the menstrual cycle and suffering particular discomfort would also benefit from calling on Maeve for assistance. Her calming energies and powers in protecting women can help ease the pain and soothe the process so it does not become debilitating.

Goddess Maeve helps with:

- Connecting to the Elementals
- Aromatherapy, herbology and healing
- Alchemy
- Beauty and attractiveness
- Strength, courage, and confidence

- Sexual prowess
- Protecting and healing horses
- Helping with the menstrual cycle

AFFIRMATION

*Thank You, Goddess Maeve, for Your
unconditional love and protection.
I am beautiful and powerful.
I am confident in my body.
I am confident of my sexuality.
I am strong and unstoppable.
I hear the Elementals.
I am a great aromatherapist.
I am a great alchemist.
I am a great herbologist.
I am a true healer.
I protect horses.
I heal horses.
I have a painless menstrual cycle.*

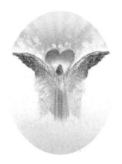

GODDESS OONAGH

A special goddess for those looking to connect with the fairy realm, Goddess Oonagh is the Queen of the Fairies. Known as one of the most beautiful of all the goddesses, Oonagh represents magic, mystery, and femininity all in one.

Goddess Oonagh connects deeply with the inner child inside each of us, encouraging us to reconnect with our young selves and to never stop believing in magic. As we get older, it is easy to lose connection with our inner child. We become so bogged down by the stresses of life and the responsibilities of adulthood that we forget there is a small child, deep inside us, who still believes in the impossible and dares to dream. Oonagh can help us find this child once again and lead us to a path of happy fruitfulness.

Known for her striking beauty, Goddess Oonagh also helps us feel beautiful about ourselves, recognising the unique beauty each one of us possesses. Those who feel unattractive, unworthy or lack in self-confidence can call upon Oonagh to help them feel confident in their own beauty. We are all different, unique, and special in our own way.

We were all blessed with a specific type of beauty and there is no one-size-fits-all when it comes to beauty. Calling upon Oonagh helps us to realise that.

Dancers, or anyone involved in the arts or movement of some kind will also benefit from this powerful, benevolent goddess. She assists those who wish to take care of their bodies, to keep them healthy and invigorated. This is why she is also excellent help to those who engage in forms of exercise. People who are suffering with issues of weight or struggling to motivate themselves to exercise and become healthier can call upon Oonagh to help them. For many, being unhappy with their body can lead to low self-esteem, which can result in 'comfort-eating', perpetuating a vicious cycle that is hard to break out of. Oonagh can help us break out of this cycle and become the best, healthiest versions of ourselves.

Oonagh is a deity of magic and, as such, she assists all those who dabble in the magical arts. She is, as previously mentioned, Queen of the Fairies and is integral to work with when contacting the fairy realm. She helps anyone who is involved in, or wishes to be involved in, a love relationship, encouraging love, loyalty, faithfulness, and trust, bringing two souls closer together so they may become one in harmonious synchronization.

Goddess Oonagh helps with:

- Feeling beautiful and attractive
- Exercise and dancing
- Motivation

- Divine magic
- Contacting the fairies
- Love relationships

AFFIRMATION

Thank You, Goddess Oonagh, for Your
unconditional love and protection.
I am beautiful.
I embrace my own beauty.
I am attractive in my own way.
Beauty is subjective.
I motivate myself.
I stick to my exercise regime.
I complete my work-out.
I eat well and become the best of myself.
I connect to the fairy realm.
I harness my own magic.
I use magic for the greater good.
I love my other half.
My other half and I are happy.
I spread love and joy to my relationships.
I am motivated.
I am beautiful.

GODDESS PELE

The Hawaiian Goddess of Fire, Pele, is also known as "She Who Shapes This Sacred Land" and even today she continues to have a powerful and influential effect on the people of Hawaii with her propensity to devour land with fire and volcanoes.

True to her name, Pele represents the dynamic energy of fire in all its glory. Hence, she is a marvellous help to all those who are struggling with motivation and reaching the goals they set for themselves. Many have grand ideas and visions about where they want to go in life, however, manifesting these ideas into reality can be challenging and downright daunting. Calling upon Pele can help bring empowerment to people and give them the necessary fire they need in their life to get up and achieve their goals.

Pele is there at the beginning, middle and end of ambition and drive. She helps those just starting out, as well as those who are in the process of reaching those goals, helping them to overcome the stumbling blocks along the way. Ambition is often marred with in-between failure, creating setbacks and lack of motivation. She can help people pick themselves up, dust themselves off and try again.

She is a goddess of passion and therefore helps to instill passion into others, particularly where life has become lacklustre and dull. As such, Pele uses the power of fire to breathe new life into people.

She helps people get their priorities in order. Becoming bogged down with too many responsibilities, duties, ideas, or plans can easily send someone into a negative spiral as they desperately try to prioritise everything, while ironically making little progress. Calling upon Goddess Pele for help is highly beneficial for people struggling to get everything in order. Her dynamic and soothing energies are wonderful in helping people go forward with confidence and verve.

Pele also helps with relationships, promoting honesty and stability. Energy is used in many different ways and when it is used for the greater good and not for selfish reasons, the rewards are great. Relationships take work and trust, and She helps the individuals involved trust one another so that communication can be open and honest.

Goddess Pele helps with:

- Empowerment
- Dynamic energy
- Goalsetting and reaching goals
- Passion
- Getting priorities in order
- Communication in relationships
- Promoting trust and honesty

AFFIRMATION

Thank You, Goddess Pele, for Your
unconditional love and protection.
I reach my goals.
I fulfil my ambitions.
I have the energy and drive to succeed.
I have the willpower to triumph.
I am an empowered being.
I get my priorities straight.
I prioritise my life.
I use passion to achieve my dreams.
I use my gifts for the greater good.
I believe in trust and honesty.
Honesty is essential to my relationship.
Open communication is essential to my
relationship.
I have a fulfilled relationship.
My relationship will triumph.
I use my personal power to help others.
I work on my dreams.
I stand my ground.
I am honest and trustworthy.

GODDESS SULIS

The Celtic Goddess, Sulis, is a Goddess of the Water, overseeing sacred springs and wells and all bodies of water used for ceremonies. The hot springs resort in England, Bath, is strongly connected to Sulis. When the Romans arrived in Britain, they called this resort Aquae Sulis, which means the Waters of Sulis. It was famed for its healing properties and even to this day, people visit the resort to benefit from the great healing and therapeutic vibes the hot springs can provide.

Sulis is famous for her gift of eyesight, both physical and spiritual. The name Sulis comes from word, 'eye', and this refers to her abilities as a prophet and a seer. Those involved with prophecy or who find themselves having abilities to see into the future can call on Sulis to help them. Sulis 'power with eyesight also applies to physical eyesight – anyone whose eyesight has become poorly or who struggles with seeing can call upon Sulis to help them, using her gifts to ease and comfort them.

Being a Goddess of Water, Sulis is naturally connected to the earth. Therefore, all aspects of gardening are strongly intertwined with Sulis.

Flowers, plants, vegetable patches, birds, chickens that lay eggs and all other things that go into the garden would benefit from blessings of Sulis, to help them grow, prosper, and thrive, creating beautiful surroundings for nature.

Sulis is a goddess of both clairvoyance and blessings, thereby helping those with these psychic abilities come to terms with their gifts and find ways to understand and utilise them to their greatest extent and for the benefit of all. When you seek a blessing on yourself or another, ask Sulis to help you do this, as she can use her energies to bring good fortune and peace to the individual or situation.

Sulis is also a goddess of wishes – place a wish and ask Sulis to grant it. When you throw a penny into a water fountain and make a wish, it is Sulis who listens to it and grants it, depending on whether the individual is wishing for the selfish means of the ego or for the higher good of the soul. A wish done while performing a ceremony with water is also highly recommended.

Goddess Sulis helps with:

- Clairvoyance
- Blessings
- Physical and spiritual eyesight
- Gardening
- Water used in ceremonies
- Wishes

AFFIRMATION

*Thank You, Goddess Sulis, for Your
unconditional love and protection.
I am profoundly clairvoyant.
I improve my eyesight.
I see things that haven't happened yet.
I understand my gifts better.
I love gardening.
I make a beautiful garden.
I help nature with my gardening.
I perform water-based ceremonies.
I wish for things that benefit myself and
mankind.
I believe in wishes.
I believe in the power of ceremony.
I am connected with nature.
I am connected with the all-seeing eye.*

GODDESS VESTA

Known as the Roman Goddess of the Hearth, the Goddess Vesta was also a Virgin Goddess, known for protecting and keeping the family home. She is the ultimate ruler of domestic life and is particularly helpful for mothers and housewives who spend much time in the family home.

A helper and protector of all the things that domestic life entails, Vesta is particularly good at helping homely individuals get their house in order and create a pleasant, peaceful space. If there is conflict or negative energy in your home, calling on Vesta to help clear it can be helpful, helping to promote clarity, harmony and understanding between everyone. Likewise, if there are negative entities lurking around, Vesta can help remove them from the premises, so you are not subconsciously affected by negative energies.

She is also helpful in keeping the flame within relationships sustained. Particularly if a couple has a packed family life and heavy schedules, it can be easy for the fire to die out and for passion to disappear. Vesta helps to reignite this passion, and keep it going at the same time.

Calling upon her for help produces information that can trickle to the subconscious, giving the individuals information about how to reignite the passion in one's relationship. This can be wonderful for couples, which helps to bridge any distance that may have been growing between them.

In addition, Vesta is also an enormous help in keeping the home protected and clearing space. Protection may be necessary from bad energy that finds its way into homes, whether from energy that the dwellers pick up from others, or conflicts that may arise or even negative entities that linger about. Stress, an increase in tension and arguments, bad moods, depression, foul behaviours and physical symptoms, such as fatigue and headaches, may all be signs that a household needs serious cleansing. Calling upon Vesta for help in this area can be wonderfully healing and therapeutic for everyone in the household. Simply asking her to cleanse the space and remove negative energy from the home can be enough to ease tensions, remove the desire for conflict and create a happy, peaceful atmosphere that everyone can enjoy.

Goddess Vesta helps with:

- Reigniting passion in relationships and keeping it going long after it has returned
- Clearing spaces within the home
- Domestic environment
- Protection from negative energies

AFFIRMATION

*Thank You, Goddess Vesta, for Your
unconditional love and protection.
I have a harmonious domestic life.
I reignite passion in my relationship.
I ensure the fire stays burning in my
relationship.
I have added protection in my home.
Conflicts are not necessary; we live in
peace.
I achieve peace and harmony in my home.
My domestic life is happy.
My relationship is full of love and
passion.
I protect my home from negative energies.
We all get along in harmony.
I am protected and my home is protected.*

GOD AENGUS

In Irish Mythology, the God Aengus is known as the God of Love and Beauty. A strikingly handsome and charming God, he is also known for bestowing youthfulness on others and also helping people to find their true loves.

Being the God of Love, he encompasses everything that comes with romantic love and passion. Music is a strong, significant part of this. It speaks to the soul and when two people who are meant to be hear the same song, it is enough for them to come together and recognise one another as soulmates.

Aengus can help ignite and re-ignite passion in relationships, especially if the flame has died out. He can help two lovers who may be weary and tired, either of life or one another, find that original spark that brought them together in the first place. Not only this, but he can help them sustain it so that the flame does not die out again. Romance does not have to be a dying part of a relationship, confined to the past and sweet memories; it can be a part of all relationships, strong and fiery as it ever was. Aengus helps couples keep romance in their lives.

He is wonderful in assisting with soulmate relationships. He can help people find their soulmate and recognise them for what they truly are when they are spotted. A soulmate relationship is not always easy; at times, it is extremely difficult, rife with challenges and obstacles, for soulmate relationships are about helping us grow and holding up a mirror so we may see our true selves, while helping us become the very best of ourselves. Calling upon Aengus can help us ease our way into these relationships and work with our soulmate to help one another be the best versions of who we are. These provide hard-hitting, impactful, and meaningful connections with others which can be truly lifechanging.

He helps us not only find and create soulmate relationships, but also protect them. He helps us see beyond what may be petty and shallow so that we can fully appreciate what a soulmate relationship is, thereby providing it with even greater protection.

God Aengus helps with:

- Romance and passion
- Music
- Finding soulmates
- Creating soulmate relationships
- Protecting soulmate
- Relationships
- Understanding and appreciating the beauty of oneself and the world

AFFIRMATION

*Thank You, God Aengus, for Your
unconditional love and protection.
I find my soulmate.
I have a meaningful relationship.
My soulmate shows me who I truly am.
I believe in romance.
I believe in passion.
Music is a way to the heart and soul.
I find my beloved through the power of
music.
I protect my soulmate.
My soulmate is a part of me.
I am a beautiful person.
The world is a beautiful place.
I find my other half.
My other half is out there waiting for me.
I am in a wonderful relationship with my
soulmate.
Passion does not have to die in my
relationship.
I re-ignite romance in my relationship.
I have passion and romance in my life.*

GOD APOLLO

The Greek God, Apollo, is one of the most well-known of the Greek Gods. He is the son of Zeus and the brother of Goddess Artemis, and he is famed for representing a number of things, such as art, poetry and music. He is known as the God of Light, as well as the God of Prophecy and Healing.

The God Apollo has great power, and throughout the ages, he has bestowed this power to mortals in need of help and assistance. He is particularly beneficial for those who want to change their health routine. Diet and exercise can be especially difficult to maintain in today's world; we are confronted by all sorts of junk foods and unhealthy lifestyles and it can be easy to fall into them, which leads to all sorts of health problems further down the line. God Apollo helps people break out of an unhealthy cycle by leading them away from a sedentary life that involves eating all manners of unhealthy products, and instead towards movement, exercise and a diet filled with body-friendly foods. He helps bring motivation to people, so they keep this lifestyle up and don't slip back into old ways when things become dull or difficult.

Apollo understands the negative impact of stress and therefore he helps bring respite from it, encouraging a happy ending from stressful situations. He represents the silver lining in the dark clouds and the light at the end of the tunnel.

As well as this, he goes deeper into the psyche, helping people discover and utilise their prophetic gifts. A friend to all psychic beings, he helps people understand their abilities rather than shy away from them. He helps psychics and clairvoyants see the path forward clearly so that they may be able to help themselves, those around them and the world at large. He can help these gifts be developed and not stifled.

God Apollo also helps mechanics and is known for helping to fix mechanical issues. If there is a problem on the road or some kind of machinery issue that needs fixing, Apollo can help provide you with the wisdom and guidance to recognise the issue and take the necessary steps to solve it, especially if this is a **DIY** problem!

God Apollo helps with:

- Healthy eating, exercise, and motivation
- Happy endings concerning difficult and stressful situations
- Gift of prophecy
- Psychic and clairvoyant abilities
- Fixing mechanical issues

AFFIRMATION

Thank You, God Apollo, for Your
unconditional love and protection.
I live a healthy lifestyle.
I eat a healthy diet.
I cut unhealthy and bad products from my
diet.
I stay motivated to exercise.
I make exercise a part of my routine.
I see the light at the end of the tunnel.
I realise stress from my life.
I am free of suffering.
I live a happy life.
All my situations are improving.
I have the gift of prophecy.
I learn to use my psychic abilities.
I use my clairvoyance to help myself and
others.
I am able to fix mechanical problems.

GOD HORUS

In Ancient Egypt, the God Horus was known as the God of the Sky, his name meaning "The one far above". Known as the protector of Egypt's ruler, it was also widely believed that the pharaoh of the time was the living incarnation of Horus himself.

Horus is particularly helpful to those who lack courage. Any situation, relationship or inner battle that requires courage and fortitude can be improved by calling upon Horus and asking him for strength to deal with whatever adversities may arise. Horus was one of the most powerful gods of Ancient Egypt and he lends his strength today to those who are struggling with bravery. Standing one's ground can be difficult. We may have ideas about who we want to be and what we want to achieve, but this can be difficult if we lack the courage to manifest this into reality. He helps people stand up to their enemies and find the strength of their convictions, no matter how difficult or unpopular those convictions may prove to be.

Horus 'powers extend to the ethereal too. He helps people find their inner wisdom and own powerful gifts.

People who are practicing the art of clairvoyance would find it beneficial to call upon Horus, as he will help bring clarity to the mind and belief in one's own abilities. He assists those who have realised the Divine power within themselves, helping them to grow and learn in abundance. More often than not, the process of harnessing one's own unique spiritual abilities is a long one; He assists in this to the best of his own abilities and does not falter in his support to those who ask for it. Psychic abilities is something we all possess; whether we choose to delve deeper into them and wield them for ourselves is our choice, but if we choose this path, then Horus is one of the best deities to ask for help and guidance.

Horus is particularly helpful for mother-son relationships, particularly if the relationship has become fractious or severed in any way. He can bring understanding and empathy to this very special bond and help bring those involved closer to one another, gently aiding the great love that exists between mother and son to become its purest form once more.

God Horus helps with:

- Clairvoyance
- Psychic abilities
- Mother and son relationships
- Courage
- The strength to stand your ground

AFFIRMATION

*Thank You, God Horus, for Your
unconditional love and protection.
I am strong and brave.
I have the strength of my convictions.
I stand by my beliefs.
I am courageous.
I achieve anything I set out to do.
I have psychic abilities and I use them.
I am profoundly Clairvoyant.
I wield my abilities for the greater good.
I love my mother.
I love my son.
I mend my relationship with my loved
one.
I am understanding to my loved one's
needs.
I am love and I focus on love.
I believe in my own unique path.*

GOD LUGH

The most powerful of all the Celtic gods, the God Lugh is known as the great Sun God who brings light into the world. His name aptly means "the shining".

A god also wisely known for arts and crafts, he is wonderful for artists and creators of all kinds. Writers, musicians, painters, sculptors – anyone who is engaged in the creative world would benefit from invoking Lugh, who can help provide inspiration and dedication. Following a creative project through to the end can be one of the hardest parts of embarking upon creative endeavours, but the God Lugh can bestow endurance and tenacity on the artist, helping them to remain consistent and continue with the project until it is completed.

Lugh is also known for divine magic. Those who practice the art of magic would find it entirely to their benefit to invoke Lugh, who can help them view their craft with clarity and wisdom. He is capable of providing them with the necessary patience and understanding needed to shape their gifts into the absolute best of what they can offer.

Being a bringer of light, Lugh is a natural healer. Those suffering from wounds inflicted on them due to painful situations can benefit a great deal from his powerful healing abilities. Whatever the situation is – job loss, a broken heart, family feuds, bullying or anything else that has caused pain and distress – calling upon Lugh's light can help heal these wounds and help the person emerge stronger and wiser than ever before. Lugh is also a great protector, providing protection against dark forces both in human and ethereal form. As a light-bringer, he also provides us with protection from ourselves. Where darkness exists in our heart, Lugh can help drive that darkness out with beams of light, simultaneously providing us with understanding of both the light and dark side of life.

He is a problem-solver and a wonderful ally to those who find themselves flummoxed, unable to see the woods for the trees. He can help people find the solution to any problem, should they choose to invoke his remarkable abilities.

God Lugh helps with:

- Artistic projects
- Alchemy
- Divine magic
- Healing from painful situations
- Protection and solutions to any problem

AFFIRMATION

*Thank you, God Lugh, for Your
unconditional love and protection.
I am an artist who creates great work.
I beat my writer's block.
I manifest my art into reality.
I transform myself and things around me.
I heal from my pain.
My heart is whole again.
I use my knowledge of suffering to help
others.
I am protected from dark forces.
I am a person of the light.
I work for the light.
I find a solution to any problem.
I have remarkable abilities.
I have a brilliant mind that loves to
create.
I navigate from any situation with ease.
Everything I want is made available to me.*

GOD SERAPIS BEY

Known as the Son of God who came to earth from Venus, Serapis Bey is known as the Great Disciplinarian. He is here to teach us that self-discipline is essential and necessary for our own pathway to ascension and our own freedom from the Ego which grips us while we are here on earth.

He is helpful for anyone who has internal battles with themselves and whoever struggles between doing what is right and what is easy. Hence, he assists those who suffer from addictions of all kinds, such as food, drugs, and sex, helping them to overcome their addictions and find the root cause which they use addiction to fulfil. Serapis Bey helps people in the battle between the Soul and the Ego, guiding them towards the path of truth and light, and away from darkness and deceit.

One cluster of people who struggle with expressing their Truth, are creative types – artists, musicians, and writers of all kinds. Those involved in the arts tend to have a 'dark side' which often threatens to overpower them, and this is because they are so closely linked with the Light that they veer too close to the Dark, as the veil between Light and Dark is incredibly thin.

Hence, it can be easy for them to sink into one or the other. Serapis Bey helps artists find the side of themselves which is pure light and helps them manifest it into creative artworks which can then be spread to everyone else, in turn helping others combat their own darkness. This is the ultimate power of Serapis Bey, the transformation of Dark into Light and the ascension to a higher state of mind.

He is likewise helpful with people who want to lose weight and get in better shape, and who lack motivation to do so. The physical body may only be the physical manifestation of us, but in this world, it means a lot to individuals and those around them. Being at one's healthiest and best helps to accelerate the path to ascension and Serapis Bey gently guides people towards becoming the best version of themselves.

Serapis Bey is also skilled with prophecy and helps to promote understanding of what is to come. He likewise promotes peace, both in oneself and around the globe, helping others understand the importance of empathy and learning to listen to one another.

Serapis Bey helps with:

- Overcoming addictions
- Artists and creative endeavours
- The path to ascension
- Communicating with God
- Exercise and motivation
- Prophecy
- Peace within oneself and for the world

AFFIRMATION

*Thank you, Serapis Bey, for Your
unconditional love and protection.
I overcome my addictions.
I satisfy my cravings with purity and light.
I complete my artistic quest.
I create great art.
I use my art for the greater good.
I find my higher self.
I am the best of myself.
I conquer my darkness and weaknesses.
I communicate clearly with God.
I listen to God.
I am in great shape.
I exercise and push myself.
I understand prophecy.
I have the wisdom to see what prophecy
is.
I am at peace.
I help the world find peace.*

GOD THOTH

Thoth was one of the most well-known of all the Egyptian Gods, and he was particularly famous for representing magic, wisdom, the moon and writing. He is also known as the god of balance, able to harmonise opposing forces as one. Because of this, he is particularly beneficial to those with the sun or rising sign of Libra.

The Thoth is a great perpetrator of Divine Magic. Those who wish to access this magic need only call on Thoth for help. Thoth can help you access the deepest side of yourself and help you see beyond any negative debris that may be holding you back; this negative debris that makes up the Ego can often prove a great obstacle in the quest to reach the Higher Self, often being confused for the Higher Self, in and of itself. By calling upon Thoth, this falsity can be washed away, leaving only purity and enlightening.

Likewise, he helps people understand their life purpose and is particularly good for university students or youths who are unsure about where they want to go in life.

Thoth is a god of the sciences, too. He helps people in Mathematics, Sacred Geometry and Teaching and Writing. Hence, he is very helpful to all people who struggle in these areas or people who lack confidence in them. Everyone has the ability to understand anything they need to. Often, it is a case of unlocking this understanding and wisdom - not that there is no possibility of understanding.

Call upon Thoth to help you understand things that seem puzzling and complicated.

Thoth is also a wonderful help for those dabbling in prophecy and divination. Being a God of Divine Magic, this of course extends to all forms of magic – prophecy being one. Prophecy can be a confusing area to delve into, but Thoth can help people view prophecy with clarity and concise confidence.

Marvellous for writers of all kinds, he brings encouragement and motivation to them, particularly when they are struggling with writer's block. Calling upon Thoth can help writers tap into the world of imagination and help manifest this art into reality.

God Thoth helps with:

- Divine magic
- Finding your life purpose
- Mathematics, Teaching and Writing
- Sacred Geometry
- Prophecy and divination
- Psychic gifts and understanding them

AFFIRMATION

*Thank You, God Thoth, for Your
unconditional love and protection.
I find the Divine Magic within me.
I use Divine Magic to improve my life.
I use Divine Magic for the greater good.
I find my life purpose.
I face my life purpose with courage.
I walk the path of my destiny.
I understand numbers and Mathematics.
I teach others.
I am taught by others.
I understand Sacred Geometry.
Prophecy is a gift I understand.
I look into the future to help the present.
I make use of my psychic abilities.
I use my psychic gifts for the greater
good.
I help others and myself with my psychic
abilities.
I love creative writing and I am a brilliant
writer.*

LORD ASHTAR

Lord Ashtar, also known as Ashtar Sheran, is an extraterrestrial being and representative of a group of beings that exist in the Universe. Lord Ashtar is a member of the Great White Brotherhood. He works with the Angelic Kingdom and works closely with Jesus and Archangel Michael. There are many people who have channelled and spoken with Ashtar. He has a mighty aura and is helpful in helping human beings understand the divine connection between Planet Earth and the rest of the Universe.

There are many beings in the Universe other than Man. Some of these beings incarnate to Earth and, specifically at this time when the world is undergoing a huge shift in consciousness, a number of these beings have come to Earth in order to help Mankind move forward and combat the dark energies that have infiltrated. If you are familiar with the terms Starseed, Indigo Children or Incarnate Angels, these are just some of the beings who have left their own home in the Universe to assist the world as it moves forward and breaks free of the chains that have clasped it for so long.

These people tend to have extremely specific missions here on Earth, though they are in human form and do not remember why they are here until it is time for them to 'wake up'.

Ashtar is particularly helpful for Starseeds and others like them because it gives them greater understanding of their purpose, particularly when they feel lost or alone (which is often). More Universe beings have incarnated on Earth than ever before as the world undergoes this dramatic shift. Ashtar also helps Mankind as an entire race understand 'aliens '- as they are more commonly known – and advises ways to have peaceful interactions with them and protecting the Earth from negative visitors or energies from other planets. He is also responsible for penetrating the core of Mankind's consciousness and providing a deeper understand of the way the world is changing.

Because of the Great Shift we are currently in, Ashtar is particularly crucial at this time. Many people may be confused; they feel in their bones something is happening, but they do not understand what it is. Ashtar is there to help bring understanding and wisdom to the situation. Much fear often accompanies individuals who don't understand what is happening, but Ashtar also helps to soothe and release this fear. Fear is a natural part of change, but it doesn't have to be that way. When you feel lost, alone or afraid, call on Ashtar to help you gain greater enlightenment and spiritual understanding.

Lord Ashtar helps with:

- Understanding and having peaceful interactions with extraterrestrial beings
- Profound understanding of the Earth's shift
- Releasing fear and providing protection
- Spiritual understanding

AFFIRMATION

*Thank You, Lord Ashtar, for Your
unconditional love and protection.
I am a child of the Universe and I seek
understanding.
I am a child of the Earth and I seek
understanding.
I am here to help and would like to know
my role.
I am here to assist the world towards a
better future.
I have the knowledge within me and need
to unlock it.
I find greater wisdom if I just ask.
I help others find their path on Earth.
I understand there are other Beings
among us and out there.
We work with the Universe, not against it.
I am fearless.
I am brave and I fulfil my purpose.*

THE SORCERER MERLIN

Known primarily for being the great and powerful magician who helped King Arthur ascend the throne of Camelot with his sword Excalibur, Merlin is also the patron of magic and sorcery who assists modern-day witches and wizards in harnessing their magical abilities and learning to trust the great gifts that linger within them.

In a day and age where witchcraft and sorcery are mocked and scoffed at, it can be hard for people with these innate talents to harness them without feeling like outsiders or "freaks." Calling upon Merlin can help the individual appreciate and honour their abilities, so they learn to cherish them as opposed to despising them.

Like the Merlin of legend, who spent much time in solitary life in the woods, the modern-day magician excels with their abilities in secret. It can be a lonely life for the one who chooses this path, but the rewards can be great and Merlin is always there to guide and assist. He helps those who go into alchemy, teaching them to trust their instincts and conscious mind as one. He also assists those who are learning about crystal work and divine magic.

Merlin helps provide strength and wisdom in these areas, so the individual is eased in.

He is also excellent assistance for people who engage in energy work and healing, helping them to have the confidence to make the best of their abilities.

Likewise, people who are gifted in prophecy or divination methods would do well to call upon Merlin for help. Anyone who is involved in the esoteric fields – such as crystal users, prophets, energy workers and Tarot readers – can learn a great deal from Merlin's infinite wisdom. The same applies to anyone with psychic gifts who wishes to delve into this mysterious side of themselves and learn to control them.

There are some who have abilities that others cannot even comprehend; shape-shifting and time-warping are extraordinary gifts, but it is not uncommon for the gifted individual to feel at a loss with what to do with them. Merlin can help a great deal in this area, guiding them along so they do not stumble blindly around, or else shut down their powers entirely. His powers and wisdom are absolute, and he desires to share them with us.

Merlin helps with:

- Crystal work
- Divine magic and Alchemy
- Protection
- Energy work and healing

- Understanding and harnessing prophecy and divination
- Assisting those with psychic gifts
- Shapeshifters and time-warpers

AFFIRMATION

*Thank You, Merlin, for Your
unconditional love and protection.
I harness my psychic gifts.
I am a magical being.
I use my powers for the greater good.
I am a skilled alchemist.
I am a great healer.
I work with energy.
I understand my gifts of prophecy.
I use divination as a tool.
I use divination to help others.
I am a student of divine magic.
I wield divine magic.
I am a shapeshifter.
I am a timewarper.
I accept my abilities.*

CONCLUSION

By the time you have reached this point, the help and assistance offered by the Archangels, Ascended Masters, Gods and Goddesses will hopefully have become an integral part of your path as you seek to find your self's core and life's purpose. It is a journey that I began and am still on. The beauty of life and the mystery of the universe calls to us every day.

They say that 2012 was an exceptional year; some even thought it would be the end of the world. And it was the end of the world – but not in the form of death and destruction; merely it marked the end of the world as we know it. It was the year that many around the globe began to "wake up" and where many people discovered they have special abilities. If you are reading this book, it is highly likely you have such abilities and wish to harness them.

Several remarkable things happened to me in 2012. The first was in March of that year. While feeling deeply saddened and depressed one night, my eyes closed as I desperately tried not to let the negative feelings overpower me, I suddenly saw a bright figure moving toward me. Despite the fact my eyes were closed, I could still "see" this figure. As the figure drew nearer, a warm tingling engulfed me, beginning from my toes, and finishing at my head. Overwhelming tremendous love and joy filled me, and I knew at that moment that everything was going to be alright.

The next morning, I felt peaceful, loved, energised, and motivated to move forward with my life.

One month later, two more incredible experiences occurred. The first was when I awoke during the witching hour, and as I left the room, I heard someone making a loud noise. Puzzled, I told myself it was my imagination and went to the bathroom. I returned to bed, curling up in my blankets and the strangest feeling came over me; I felt a sudden urge to turn around and, there, to my amazement, numerous stars glittered on my blanket and all over my hands. They burned brightly, just like the stars of the Milky Way; I was fully awake, and my third eye was fully opened. What I was seeing was magical; words cannot describe it. This was one of my many conformations that my abilities are real and it OK to go forward with these abilities because they had been given to me for a reason.

My third experience was one that cemented my belief firmly for good. Not long after I had met the stars, I went to get a glass of water in the kitchen. To my amazement, I saw rainbow-coloured lights on my fridge. At first, I thought it might just be a reflection until I realised no reflection could make such colours. Instinctively, I knew that the Archangels were with me. That was when voices appeared; multiple voices, all of them chattering excitedly. I asked them to please speak up, and they did. It was the voices of all my loved ones who had crossed over. Tears filled my eyes as I felt them all around me, hearing their words. The love I felt was incredible. They were so excited and happy to be talking to me, just as I was to hear them.

We must never doubt the experiences we have, just as we must never doubt our abilities. The faith we have in our gifts paves the way for other realms and other beings to open up to us. By harnessing our gifts, we can then do good in this world, in our own lives, the lives of our loved ones and the world at large.

Reading through this book, you will have learned a bit about the various deities you can call upon when you need wisdom or guidance. If you feel a little lost about where to begin or how to know if a deity is with you, don't worry at all. It is perfectly normal to feel like that at first. Everyone's experience is different, and there are many ways that Archangel, Ascended Master, God/Goddess will make themselves known to you. I will tell you another experience I had which was particularly potent.

One day I decided to visit Stonehenge. It was a place I had always wanted to visit; the energy of this ancient monument in Wiltshire was powerful and potent, and I had felt drawn to it for a long time. The night before my trip, I took a bath relaxing in the tub, a vision of a man appeared before me. He had a long beard and ancient wisdom about him. I knew that this man was Merlin and that he was waiting for me, confirming to me that the time was right for me to visit.

During my trip to Stonehenge, the wind was fierce, so fierce that I was disappointed by the end of my tour, which only took an hour. With such ferocious gales, I found it impossible to meditate and connect with the energy. Realising that attempts to connect were futile, I resigned myself to instead return in summer when the winds were not loud and distracting. Meditation requires peace and quiet, so how on earth was I meant to connect with the energy here with such gales blustering in my ears?

Instead, I decided to take pictures of the monument and various rocks. And it was then that the remarkable happened. As I was taking pictures, I started to see images on the rocks. The first was of the letter, "M", and I knew it meant "M" for Merlin. The next rock appeared the image of a man— tall, strong, powerful, and handsome. At first, I thought it was Archangel Michael, but I then realised it was King Arthur. The next rock was of a breathtakingly beautiful woman - this was Queen Guinevere. The rock after that had Merlin himself - just as in my vision the night before, he was not very tall, he wore a red cape and had a long white beard.

Others appeared too who were not part of Arthurian legend. The Goddess, Aphrodite, showed herself to me; she was stunning; the front of her body was clouded in white roses, while her back remained naked. The next rock had a male and female with a tree between them; later, I discovered this was Adam and Eve, and the Tree of Life. On the final rock, multiple people were celebrating something; they were dancing, I could see the interactions, the movement and happiness; truly beautiful. It was like watching a movie.

At that moment, the greatest joy and happiness filled my heart. My clairvoyance was profound. Any residue of doubt that had previously lingered washed away from me. King Arthur, Guinevere, Merlin, Aphrodite, Adam, Eve, and the dancing people had guided me to Stonehenge to let me know that my gifts were real. I also felt this was a reward, and every gift I possessed had been given to me for a reason. A purpose that I now understood with greater clarity than I have ever before. And I am grateful for my gifts!

That is why I have written this book for you, dear reader. I want you to know that you are not alone, no matter who or where you are in the world. No matter what you are going through or how lost or afraid you may become, you can call upon the Archangels, Ascended Masters, Gods and

Goddesses to assist you. We all have different path and experiences in life. Our journey to self-discovery and enlightenment it's a unique one for the individual. You can invoke them using the information in this book, or you can call on them in whatever way feels right for you. This book is a source of inspiration, freedom, healing, acknowledgement of the Beings around us and how they can help you. Above all, you will become who you were born to be; a source of light and love in the lives of yourself and those around you.

As Divine Beings, we are on an evolutionary and transformational journey, and we are loved unconditionally.

I love you, and God bless you!

Made in the USA
Las Vegas, NV
09 June 2021